The sun slowly rises

The sun slowly rises

Readings, reflections and prayers for Holy Week
from the Iona Community

Neil Paynter

wild goose
publications  www.**ionabooks**.com

Contributions copyright © the individual contributors
Compilation copyright © Neil Paynter

Published 2017 by
Wild Goose Publications
21 Carlton Court, Glasgow G5 9JP, UK,
the publishing division of the Iona Community.
Scottish Charity No. SC003794. Limited Company Reg. No. SC096243.

ISBN 978-1-84952-527-5

Cover photo © David Coleman

The publishers gratefully acknowledge the support of the Drummond Trust,
3 Pitt Terrace, Stirling FK8 2EY in producing this book.

All rights reserved. Apart from the circumstances described below relating to non-commercial use, no part of this publication may be reproduced in any form or by any means, including photocopying or any information storage or retrieval system, without written permission from the publisher.

Non-commercial use: The material in this book may be used non-commercially for worship and group work without written permission from the publisher. If photocopies of small sections are made, please make full acknowledgement of the source, and report usage to the CLA or other copyright organisation.

Neil Paynter has asserted his right in accordance with the Copyright, Designs and Patents Act, 1988, to be identified as the author of this work.

Overseas distribution
Australia: Willow Connection Pty Ltd, Unit 4A, 3–9 Kenneth Road, Manly Vale, NSW 2093
New Zealand: Pleroma, Higginson Street, Otane 4170, Central Hawkes Bay
Canada: Bayard Distribution, 10 Lower Spadina Ave., Suite 400, Toronto, Ontario M5V 2Z

Printed by Bell & Bain, Thornliebank, Glasgow

Contents

Readings, reflections and prayers for Holy Week

Introduction, Neil Paynter   7

Palm Sunday: Surges of hope, Katharine M Preston   13

Monday of Holy Week: The courage to be the only voice, Lyn Ma   19

Tuesday of Holy Week: 'Peace will grow from the ground up', Mike Mineter   25

Wednesday of Holy Week: An extravagant gift of love, Bonnie Thurston   31

Maundy Thursday: In the shadows, Elaine Gisbourne   39

Good Friday: The veil of the temple, Stephen Wright   47

Holy Saturday: In our 'not there yet' world, Marie Pattison   55

Easter Sunday: God rolls away the stones, John McCall   61

Resources for Holy Week

Prayers for the journey to Easter (from Maundy Thursday to Easter Sunday), Elaine Gisbourne   68

Crucifixion 2017-style, Paul Nicolson   74

My love is like a red, red rose, Brian Quail   75

'This is my child', Anna Briggs   77

'May peace prevail': An interview with Lyn Ma, Lyn Ma and Neil Squires   78

You – yes – you: A meditation on Simon of Cyrene, Alison Swinfen   82

Prayers on crucifixion, David Rhodes   84

Take us back: Good Friday worship on the words from the Cross,
David McNeish   90

Your life in us: Prayers on the seven words from the Cross, Peter Millar   97

Holy Week poems, Bonnie Thurston   101

We Will Tread the Earth Lightly: A service of lamentation to liberate us for
action, Chris Polhill   105

The disturbing and good news (Holy Saturday on Iona),
Thom M Shuman   115

Easter Sunday sermon from Iona Abbey, Nicola Slee   119

Love that breaks open stone: Poems for Easter Sunday, Alison Swinfen   124

Night sight, Elaine Gisbourne   129

Invisible guests, John McCall   131

The ten Beatitudes, Alastair McIntosh   133

The incredible love of God in Christ, Ian M Fraser   137

Sources and acknowledgements   141

About the authors   143

Introduction

A story of resurrection (from before digital cameras) …

'People ask me how I can always be so happy,' says Gary, and tells me his story. About how some junkies broke into his basement room and stole his TV and music system. Stabbed him in the head and ribs sixteen times.

'I thought I was falling asleep, but I was really dying.'

'During it I had this feeling,' he says. 'Like someone suddenly reached out and touched me. My guardian angel, my mum said. And I knew I was safe and held in love.'

Sunlight falls on Gary's face and he closes his eyes; he says the stabbing helped to clear away the fog. 'People ask me how I can always be so happy – I'm back from death.'

He looks like he's on permanent vacation – standing in flowery knee-length shorts, leather sandals, and a T-shirt proclaiming LIFE'S A BEACH; a great smile across his broad tanned face.

We're standing in the middle of the city sidewalk. People run to important meetings; wait with clouded looks. Gary's bopping and dancing away …

I remind him about the last time I saw him. Down at the drop-in – pale and shivering in a corner, hugging himself.

'Ya, I wasn't a pretty picture, eh?'

Gary tells me he's moved and hardly ever goes there now. He likes to go on long walks – round the park, the market, the botanical gardens … He's got energy to burn – energy he never knew he had.

'Here, look,' he says, and shows me the camera his father sent him for his birthday, turns it over in his knuckly hands like treasure. He laughs: 'I used to hate people taking *my* picture. I used to think I was ugly. Ugly from the inside out, you know? Now I wear my shorts, take my shirt off. Why not?' he says, and opens the zoom lens, 'there's nothin' to be ashamed of.'

Gary doesn't care if people see his scars, or think he's crazy or stupid.

'God thinks I'm beautiful. Jesus calls me his beloved son,' he says, like he has stood in front of God's gaze and grown bright with it. Like something brilliant has happened, and he'll never feel ashamed again.

I ask him what he likes to take photos of, and he says people he loves, things he loves: 'Sunsets and sunrises. Squares and fountains. Faces and flowers ... I used to sit and watch TV. Now I wanna take pictures.'

Gary says he loves the way the light changes – and is everywhere. 'There's so much I never even noticed before. You know? ... So, that's why I listen to jazz,' he says, and excitedly shows me his Walkman now. 'I used to listen to basement music – Black Sabbath, Iron Maiden. Now I listen to jazz. Walk around everyplace and take pictures and listen to jazz ... I used to hate it. I didn't understand. The joy. The joy, but sadness too. Jazz people went through a lot, suffered. But it's the joy that comes through stronger in the end – Louis Armstrong, Ella Fitzgerald. I listen to the words. I never did before. They sink in. I used to hate it. I used to hate everything ... Life was a bitch. I didn't understand.'

Gary shrugs. 'Sometimes you gotta die to be born,' he says, and starts showing me the stack of photos he keeps in his backpack, with a bottle of water; drops one the wind catches and carries off. 'Oh well, someone'll find it,' he laughs, as it Spirits away.

Gary says he was dead. Dead when they climbed in his casket and stole his buried treasure. Now his treasure is the light that glitters. Each new day. 'I just thank God ... See, *listen*,' he says, and reaches up and lays his hands on me: gives me his headphones.

'Can you hear? ...... See – light and dark. Sorrow and joy ... Can you hear?' he trumpets. People passing glance round, wondering if he's talking to them. I listen. And can hear: the bluesy key, the brassy joy.

While I'm listening to the music of life, Gary stands out on the street corner handing out his photographs: waxy, shiny leaves of grass breaking up through concrete; blazing heads of flowers in a litter-strewn wasteland; the sun slowly rising up over office towers and apartment blocks ... Gives one to a woman who stops, taken aback ... then smiles as something slowly sinks in. Hands one to a man who lights up and laughs. He seems to know who to give them to: people stopped or slowed with care or worry; folk in a hurry who only have time for a bite. He seems to know: who needs energy, who needs some hope. I close my eyes – and can see pictures in the music ...

I hand him back his halo.

Gary says when he walks through the mean street valley now he feels protected; he smiles, the lines and wrinkles around his eyes all crinkly and radiating out.

He looks lit up from within – his face beaming, his Hawaiian shorts like stained glass glowing.

The sun's out and the world is full of light. It seems to me that Gary is making it that way – and he is. We shake hands and he strolls off, listening to the sea of life.

I watch him disappear down the street, taking pictures of everything in the world he nearly lost.

Heading uptown everything is lit up from within. The crucified, leafy trees; the lined faces of souls ... Like a saint has passed this way trailing and spreading light. Like the fog has cleared.

There's a smell of tar; dazzle and glitter of sand dunes on a building site.

There's a gentle breeze and a warm, embracing feeling – I can feel the sun, sinking into my bones and heart. I want to run home and put my shorts on!

So why are you *so happy?* people passing seem to ask. *I'm back from death ...*

The sun slowly rises
on the streets of Toronto
where saints trail and spread God's light

10   The Sun Slowly Rises

The sun slowly rises
at Standing Rock
in the Dakotas

The sun slowly rises
in Glasgow classrooms
where folk teach English as a second language to refugees and asylum seekers
from Guinea, Ivory Coast, Congo, Eritrea,
Sudan, Syria, Iran, Iraq, China, Vietnam ...
and people come to understand
we are all one

The sun slowly rises
at islands for world peace in Dumfries
and over Iona Abbey

The sun slowly rises
on farms in Palestine
where folk plant olive trees
and work to grow peace
from the ground up

The sun slowly rises
in food pantries
in West Virginia

The sun slowly rises in all the everyday
and extravagant
gifts of caring
poured out for Jesus and his friends

*The sun slowly rises
in Lancaster
in the stinking shadows between the cinema
and Wetherspoon's
where street pastors hand out bandages and love*

*The sun slowly rises
in houses of hospitality in Cumbria
and Salford*

*The sun slowly rises
everywhere people work together to build
a 'church of the poor'.*

*The sun slowly rises in Spirit-filled churches everywhere from Taipei
to Orkney*

*The sun slowly rises in BBQ restaurants in Malaysia
where folk from many countries work together,
and gather at breaks to talk about
their lives and dreams and faith*

*The sun slowly rises
at demos in Tottenham
in solidarity with those suffering
unjust taxation and benefit cuts*

*The sun slowly rises at climate marches around the globe
and in Resurrection gardens
in Cannock Wood*

The Sun Slowly Rises

*The sun slowly rises
at Faslane submarine base
where protesters sing and waltz
the dance of life
and blockade death
and pray for the day when
all nuclear weapons are abolished*

The sun slowly rises …

*Feel it on your face and hands and
in your heart
Spring is coming*

*The light shines in the darkness
and the darkness will never put it out*

In the early dawn they went to the tomb …

The sun slowly rises …

Neil Paynter, Biggar, Scotland, Lent 2017

Palm Sunday
Surges of hope

Katharine M Preston

Bible reading: Mark 11:1–10 (NIV)

As they approached Jerusalem and came to Bethphage and Bethany at the Mount of Olives, Jesus sent two of his disciples, saying to them, 'Go to the village ahead of you, and just as you enter it, you will find a colt tied there, which no one has ever ridden. Untie it and bring it here. If anyone asks you, "Why are you doing this?" say, "The Lord needs it and will send it back here shortly."'

They went and found a colt outside in the street, tied at a doorway. As they untied it, some people standing there asked, 'What are you doing, untying that colt?' They answered as Jesus had told them to, and the people let them go. When they brought the colt to Jesus and threw their cloaks over it, he sat on it. Many people spread their cloaks on the road, while others spread branches they had cut in the fields. Those who went ahead and those who followed shouted,

'Hosanna!'

'Blessed is he who comes in the name of the Lord!'

'Blessed is the coming kingdom of our father David!'

'Hosanna in the highest heaven!'

Reflection: Surges of hope

Celebration! Jesus rides into Jerusalem on a donkey, throngs of people cheering. Their deepest, long-submerged hopes for change – any possible change in light of occupying forces – bubble to the surface at the sight of this man who heals and comforts, and also teaches a radical change of view, rattling the uneasy domestic peace. They wave palm branches, symbols of victory, and set them on the road into Jerusalem.

When I first saw the flags and poles decorated with bright ribbons and feathers being waved in jubilation by the horse-riding Dakota Sioux youth at Standing Rock, North Dakota, and heard the hurrahs of celebration, I could not help but be reminded of Palm Sunday. The decision by a federal government agency to delay construction on an oil pipeline threatening the local water source might be only temporary, but it was a radical change from the status quo. After 500 years of occupation, the United States government stepped back, at least a little.

Surges of hope, shattering the surrounding darkness, providing a glimpse of a radical alternative. Even if brief, even if the following minutes, hours, days are unknown and scary, the surge of hope carries us forward.

Hope is audacious, says Barack Obama. Audacity implies a risk (you might be wrong) as well as a certain impudence (you are bucking the prevailing view). Within this telling ambiguity, hope quickens the heart with maybe just a twinge of fear.

But we embrace hope. Without these surges of hope – however brief – how can we continue on the path to Jerusalem? How can we endure the occupying forces winning yet once again, denying our deep connections to the land and the waters flowing over and under it?

Without surges of hope, how can the world endure the spectre of four or maybe even eight years of an inconceivable tangle of justice-scorning, science-denying, equity-slashing and peace-threatening moves on the part of the United States government?

Surges of hope are felt in the gut and in the heart. The more quiet, private instances can be prompted by a little green hump of a pea-shoot emerging from the soil in our garden on a spring day; hearing the first notes of a cherished piece of music coming through on the radio; a better-than-expected medical test result; a callback for a second interview; a handwritten note from someone we would very much like to get to know better. In each case, the heart-centre of our soul bursts out with a little smile.

Surges of hope can be ignited by prophecy fulfilled. For the people lining the streets toward Jerusalem, a scriptural text from Zachariah heightened their anticipation:

> *Rejoice greatly, Daughter Zion!*
> *Shout, Daughter Jerusalem!*
> *See, your king comes to you,*
> *righteous and victorious,*
> *lowly and riding on a donkey,*
> *on a colt, the foal of a donkey.*
> *(Zachariah 9:9, NIV)*

Surges of hope are stored in the corridors of our memories, balm against tough times: Nelson Mandela walking out the gates of prison in Cape Town; the historic handshake between the Queen of England and Deputy First Minister Martin McGuinness of Northern Ireland; the declaration by the newscasters at 11:00pm on November 4, 2008 that a black man was to be the next President of the United States.

'Hope is that thing inside us that insists, despite all evidence to the contrary, that something better awaits us if we have the courage to reach for it, and to work for it, and to fight for it,' said that President.[1]

We are deep in 'all evidence to the contrary' these days. It is hard for us in America, and I suspect for many others throughout the world, not to despair at the challenges of insular populism, ultra-nationalism, rising levels of carbon in the atmosphere, fundamentalism of many kinds fuelled by fear, not to mention a United States of America that in these times seems possessed by underlying malevolence.

So we search for signs: a victory celebration at Standing Rock; the Eiffel Tower and Arc de Triomphe lit up with green light in honour of the Paris Climate Agreement; the image of a rolled-up-shirt-sleeved Prime Minister Justin Trudeau bending down to smile and shake hands with a Syrian refugee child, one of almost 40,000 welcomed so far into Canada.

And one day in January of this very year, millions upon millions of people marching all over the world on behalf of women, many wearing the most ridiculous pink hats with ears …

We need to focus on the Palm Sundays in our lives. And we need to shout more, take to the streets, cheering, pointing out to others along the road: 'Look what is happening! This is new! This is different! This is hopeful!'

The surges of hope are simply the sparks that light the tinder. Sustaining hope is hard work. The flame needs oxygen and great care to keep it burning, to help it light up the world. There are crosses to bear, bridges to cross, justice to uphold.

'Hope is believing in spite of the evidence and then watching the evidence change,' says Jim Wallis of the Sojourners community.[2] Not just watch: we must *commit* ourselves to make the change. *We* must provide the evidence. There are many

causes. Each of us must figure out how we will move forward.

We are in a singular time of change. Old practices, old assumptions, especially about government, are being challenged. We are still trying to figure out what it all means; the path often remains indistinct and frightening at times. But the signposts – surges of hope – are strategically stationed by God to guide us. Watch for them. Listen. This *is* the way! Praise God, and shout Hosanna!

Sources:
1. From Barack Obama's Iowa caucus victory speech, January 3, 2008
2. Paraphrase of Hebrews 11:1

Prayer

Dear epiphany-loving God:

we see you in the emerging pea-shoot in spring
and in the sublime tableaux of distant mountains,
in the love gaze of a child,
the healing of a misunderstanding
or the feeding of the hungry.
Help us also to be open to the blossoming of hope that comes
in an unexpected ray of you
shining through the expected,
the usual,
the conventional –
breaking open our hearts with joy.

We ask in the name of Jesus,
the man who still astonishes us.
Amen

Monday of Holy Week
The courage to be the only voice

Lyn Ma

Bible reading: Matthew 25:35–40 (NIV)

'For I was hungry and you gave me something to eat, I was thirsty and you gave me something to drink, I was a stranger and you invited me in, I needed clothes and you clothed me, I was sick and you looked after me, I was in prison and you came to visit me.'

Then the righteous will answer him, 'Lord, when did we see you hungry and feed you, or thirsty and give you something to drink? When did we see you a stranger and invite you in, or needing clothes and clothe you? When did we see you sick or in prison and go to visit you?'

The King will reply, 'Truly I tell you, whatever you did for one of the least of these brothers and sisters of mine, you did for me.'

Reflection: The courage to be the only voice

Jerusalem. The seat of power. The place where decisions are made and the loudest voices are listened to. Where terror is used to control and oppress. The powerful like to show their power, so no one can doubt who is in charge.

But yesterday you came into Jerusalem riding on a donkey, hearing the crowds and cheers welcoming you into the city. The palm-waving and the hosannas. You must have been left with the noise of it all ringing in your ears.

Yet those who said they loved you and understood what you were trying to do were soon too scared to stand with you.

Too scared to stand up for you; even to be seen with you.

It is easy when everyone is on your side. Far harder to be the only voice, the one who stands out in the crowd.

You embraced those who were different and spoke up for those who were outcast, even when it meant you were in danger from those who tried to stop you.

We all want to be accepted, and so we surround ourselves with those we know and understand and who are like us. Yet unless we step out of what is comfortable, take the risk to meet those who are not like us, we will never see the truth. The truth that whatever the colour of our skin, or the language that comes from our lips or the name we give to our God – we are all the same.

You knew that love is what unites us, and that love is the only thing that lasts. Love can ride the waves of hope and the depths of despair. Love has the power to move us to act with compassion. Love calls us to walk the path of peace and to seek light in deepest darkness.

When we turn on our TVs and look at the faces of those who have travelled across deserts and seas, in the backs of lorries and in inflatable boats meant for 20 but with 200 people holding on with every last ounce of strength, what do we see? From the fortunate places we find ourselves in, what are we moved to do? Are we brave enough to raise our voices and open our hearts and shout that love is stronger than hate? To embrace those who are different to us? To make our voices heard, and to keep shouting – even when we are scared, even when we have to challenge the mighty and powerful? Do we have the courage to be the only voice? …

> *I see your eyes full of fear,*
> *and I cannot begin to know what those eyes have seen.*
> *You smile nervously and I smile back.*
> *I am anxious to show you that I care,*
> *that with me you can feel safe and secure.*
>
> *You tell me 'I am broken'.*
> *I hear those words*
> *and I see the pain and the loss*
> *etched across your face.*
> *I need humility to help me understand.*
> *We need a relationship based on equality.*
> *Not one where I 'fix' you.*
> *Not one where you learn my language,*
> *my culture*
> *and I make no effort to understand yours.*
> *This journey we are on together is not short.*
> *It takes time and courage.*
> *It takes tenacity.*
> *And each image of drowned bodies on a beach,*

weary people walking,
people shivering in flimsy tents,
calls me not to turn away and harden my heart.
To say I can't take any more –
I'm already doing what I can.
They call me to shout,
to raise my voice,
to challenge those in power
to act with love and compassion
and not fear and hate.

Let me have the courage to stand with you
and stand for you.
Let me use my place of privilege
to act in ways that show that
what we have in common
is far greater than
what makes us different.

Let me believe that love has power,
a power that can change hearts,
change minds,
and give me courage to stand face to face
with those who are broken
and know I am broken too.
Let me not stand silent.

For an interview with Lyn Ma about her work with refugees and asylum seekers, go to 'May peace prevail' in the Resource section, p.78.

Tuesday of Holy Week

'Peace will grow from the ground up'

Mike Mineter

Bible reading: Luke 19:37–42 (NIV)

When he came near the place where the road goes down the Mount of Olives, the whole crowd of disciples began joyfully to praise God in loud voices for all the miracles they had seen:

'Blessed is the king who comes in the name of the Lord!'

'Peace in heaven and glory in the highest!'

Some of the Pharisees in the crowd said to Jesus, 'Teacher, rebuke your disciples!'

'I tell you,' he replied, 'if they keep quiet, the stones will cry out.'

As he approached Jerusalem and saw the city, he wept over it and said, 'If you, even you, had only known on this day what would bring you peace …'

Reflection: 'Peace will grow from the ground up'

'So, when did you learn about olive trees?' I was asked.

'I've been doing it for all my life as a woodsman – ever since I began caring for trees … that would be, let me think … yes, this morning.' I discounted the time my pal Brian and I helped dad trim a diseased apple tree, and cut the wrong branch off.

I was visiting the Tent of Nations (www.tentofnations.org) a few miles outside of Bethlehem in the West Bank. Here the Nassar family runs an educational and environmental farm which welcomes volunteers *'to help build bridges between people, and between people and the land'*. I was indeed getting close to the land, and the trees. I was less keen on getting close to the donkey manure to be spread around them. But even that grew on me – especially when I got downwind of it.

I became fond of the olive trees … I was trimming the errant lowest branches so the trees would grow well. It was an easy metaphor for, and expression of, prayer for Palestine and for myself. 'Like the trees, peace will grow from the ground up,' I was told. I remembered hearing, time and again in different places in the Holy Land, Palestinians say, 'Of course the settlers will stay; we would not turn them out as many have now known nowhere else. We just want equality and justice, an end to occupation and oppression. There is plenty of space for Palestinians and Israelis.' At Tent of Nations, the principle is that *'faced with great injustice, we know that we should not hate, despair, or flee. We can refuse to be enemies and channel our pain and frustration into positive actions which will build a better future.'*

It was a delight to be on that land and with those trees, but such connections are now denied to so many Palestinians. From the hilltop, every view was past Israeli settlements, which overnight cast their harsh orange glow. The stars and so many more of creation's gifts were hidden. Under occupation, it is even illegal for Palestinians to collect rainwater; the water supplies and electricity grid that pass so close by are, like some roads, the 'sterile' ones, unavailable to Palestinians.

Olive trees are symbols of life, land and community. They grow slowly. Some of the oldest in Palestine, which had been passed down from generation to generation, were uprooted and destroyed when the Separation Barrier was built. Others are now inaccessible. I heard it claimed that some in the Garden of Gethsemane, on the Mount of Olives, were 2000 years old.

Up the hill from the Garden of Gethsemane is the teardrop-shaped Church of Dominus Flevit, commemorating Jesus' weeping over the fate of Jerusalem. The view through plain-glass, lead-framed windows is of the Kidron Valley, and beyond to the Old City of Jerusalem. Gazing through the window, the stones that came to my mind were ones that shouted, but not in praise: more than 1000 'Palestinian-owned structures' had been seized or demolished in 2016, according to OCHA (the UN Office of the Coordination of Humanitarian Affairs).[1]

I pondered where I had felt most in touch with the Resurrection on this journey: not in the huge clericalised Church of the Holy Sepulchre – but with people who, while being so oppressed, had reaffirmed in word and deed that we can only be human together; with those who focused on making a difference now, where they are.

Prayer

*I pray for these people,
that their faith, hope and courage
be sustained.
I pray for more miracles in this land of miracles:
that there be respect for all its people,
that the earth's resources be shared,
that the dark oppression of the occupation fades
with the dawn of a new era.*

*I pray that this Easter
I might be drawn a little further
outside my comfort zone to
in some small way
engage in,
not merely observe,
struggles for justice and integrity.*

*I pray that the barriers we encounter in ourselves
and in our communities
might be overcome
by a renewed closeness to Christ.*

Source:
1. www.ochaopt.org/theme/destruction-of-property

Wednesday of Holy Week
An extravagant gift of love

Bonnie Thurston

Bible reading: Mark 14:1–11 (NRSV)

It was two days before the Passover and the festival of Unleavened Bread. The chief priests and the scribes were looking for a way to arrest Jesus by stealth and kill him; for they said, 'Not during the festival, or there may be a riot among the people.'

While he was at Bethany in the house of Simon the leper, as he sat at the table, a woman came with an alabaster jar of very costly ointment of nard, and she broke open the jar and poured the ointment on his head. But some were there who said to one another in anger, 'Why was the ointment wasted in this way? For this ointment could have been sold for more than three hundred denarii, and the money given to the poor.' And they scolded her. But Jesus said, 'Let her alone; why do you trouble her? She has performed a good service for me. For you always have the poor with you, and you can show kindness to them whenever you wish; but you will not always have me. She has done what she could; she has anointed my body beforehand for its burial. Truly I tell you, wherever the good news is proclaimed in the whole world, what she has done will be told in remembrance of her.'

Then Judas Iscariot, who was one of the twelve, went to the chief priests in order to betray him to them. When they heard it, they were greatly pleased, and promised to give him money. So he began to look for an opportunity to betray him.

Reflection: An extravagant gift of love

In Mark's carefully organised gospel, the last week of Jesus' life is the most carefully organised narrative. We can follow the temporal structure of a week in Mark 11:1 to 16:8 because the evangelist calls attention to the days. Mark 11:1–11, Jesus' entry into Jerusalem, precedes 'On the following day' (11:12), one which includes the related fig tree and temple episodes. Mark 11:20 opens Tuesday ('In the morning'), an exhausting day of discourses and controversy, happily followed on Wednesday (14:1, 'two days before the Passover') by an act of extravagant love. Thursday (14:12, 'the first day of Unleavened Bread') holds the preparations for Passover, the Last Supper, Gethsemane, arrest, and Jesus' trial before the Sanhedrin. Friday (15:1, 'As soon as it was morning'), which we call 'Good Friday' and Arab Christians, perhaps more accurately, call 'Sad Friday', is the day of Jesus' trial before Pilate, condemnation, crucifixion, and burial. On Saturday (15:42, 'When evening had come') everything stopped. Silence. Emptiness. Sunday (16:1, 'When the Sabbath was over') the spice-bearing women learn of Jesus' resurrection.

New Testament commentaries discuss the complex problems of dating. But ordinary readers of Mark experience Wednesday as a day of extravagant love. The dark story of controversy, misunderstanding, betrayal, unjust legal proceedings, abandonment, torture, public humiliation and death is bisected by an act of extraordinary, selfless love. Mark uses his characteristic framing device, an 'inclusion', to tell the story. Mark 14:1–2 reveals that in the most holy time of Passover religious officials seek a way to arrest and kill Jesus. Mark 14:10–11 tells us that, for a fee, Judas Iscariot cooperates with those plans. These intrigues frame 14:3–9 and highlight the story of an anonymous woman and her loving, prophetic action.

In Bethany (literally 'House of Ananiah', house of the poor or afflicted) Jesus reclines (suggesting a feast) at table with a leper, an excluded person, when another marginal character, a woman, enters with a jar of 'pure nard', a costly plant perfume from India. Since one broke off the neck of such a jar to open it, its whole contents were used, a point not lost on the other dinner guests who, in the 'house of the poor', thought better use could have been made of what amounted to a year's wages. The (male?) disciples and dinner guests scold or rebuke (the word literally means something like 'snort in anger at') the woman. Characteristically, Jesus sees things differently. In verses 5–7, he suggests that 'practical' use of funds may not always be the best use of them. (When we have difficulty raising money for good and just causes, this is difficult to remember.) In Mark's narrative, Jesus had recently said that one who wants 'to be first among you must be slave of all' (Mark 10:44). It was slave work to anoint house guests.

What Jesus sees is a woman who deeply understood what it means to be his disciple, the focus of Mark chapters 8–10. Perhaps this woman was one who 'used to follow him and provided for him when he was in Galilee', who had heard his teaching, and 'who had come up with him to Jerusalem' (Mark 15:41). In the company of his colleagues, Jesus takes the part of the woman (imagine that, my sisters!), thereby (in a shame and honour culture) shaming the attendant men. In other accounts of this event (especially John 12:1–8) the evangelists stress the great sensuality of the action (which may intensify the diners' shock). But there is no indication that Jesus objects to being touched, to receiving an action of care for his body. Flesh is not to be despised, but honoured. (Note: 'honoured' not 'worshipped'.) Finally, Jesus sees in the woman's gesture of love prophetic action. The dinner guests don't see beyond the material; Jesus sees the spiritual implications. In his day kings were anointed, and priests – and corpses. 'She has anointed my body beforehand for burial' (14:8).

What the woman has done apparently confirms what Jesus has suspected. And it echoes another story about a generous woman which was also preceded by a critique of religious officialdom (12:35–40 and 41–44). The story, often called 'the widow's mite', follows one in which Jesus warns against ostentation and unhealthy craving for position, against false piety, attempts to cover greed by outward displays of devotion, hypocrisy to hide injustice. That account also closes with Jesus' commendation of an anonymous woman: 'she out of her poverty has put in everything she had, all she had to live on' (12:44).

These stories occur in the last week of Jesus' life. What the generous widow did prefigured Jesus' own self-giving. He, too, put in his whole life. Shortly thereafter, the anointing woman seems the first person in Mark's narrative really to understand that Jesus is the Messiah, the soon to be sacrificed Messiah. What the anointing woman does confirms his impending death, symbolically crowns him king, anoints him for burial, and prefigures the work of the spice-bearing women who find the tomb empty (16:1–8). Jesus' life message and his incipient passion are encapsulated in this Bethany encounter.

Holy Week, the last week of our Lord's life, is a difficult one on which to accompany him. (As if all the others weren't!) Perhaps this is why many Christian traditions more or less ignore it, passing from Palm Sunday's 'triumphal entry' (some scholarship suggests it might not have been exactly that) directly to Easter Sunday. This conveniently excludes the struggles of the last week that Mark and the other evangelists so carefully record. Christian life does not proceed from triumph to triumph. In following Jesus there is a lot of being hungry, angry and confronted, a lot of wandering around in the unfamiliar, dirty places, of being misunderstood by one's friends, family and religious authorities. When we try to walk with Jesus we may find ourselves in the midst of the sort of ugly plotting that frames the anointing woman's story. And Jesus' week (and sometimes our good work?) seems to end on Friday at Golgotha.

And yet. And yet. At the centre of Mark's narrative of Jesus' last week is this extraordinary story which is so full of consolation. Jesus had friends in Bethany.

(John 11, and in light of it, Luke 10:38–42 confirm this.) Ironically, in a place named for poverty and affliction, and the house of a person many would exclude, Jesus finds friendship and table fellowship (even if it is among people who, like us, can be remarkably uncomprehending of what is really going on beneath appearances). At the temporal centre of the darkness and difficulty of Passion Week, there is an experience of fellowship that must have been for Jesus solace for body and spirit. His friends had him over for a meal. Somebody cared for him with individuated, extravagant and exacting attention. Somebody 'got it', realised, however obliquely, who he was and where he was headed.

At the centre of Holy Week is an illuminated-by-the-darkness-that-surrounds-it act of extravagant love. It brings into brilliant focus what Jesus has been doing throughout his ministry: pouring out his life for his friends. What the anointing woman does, is what Jesus does: she pours out her life for her friend. It is a relief to arrive at Wednesday of Holy Week, a respite from the ugliness and suffering of it. But it also offers again what is for Mark's Jesus the great challenge of discipleship: to make of our capabilities, weaknesses and failures (yes, these too), our resources, and our very lives, an extravagant gift of love for others (especially those in desperately difficult circumstances) and, through them, for Jesus, himself.

The anonymous, anointing woman knew what is required of disciples is extravagant love at the centre. Of everything. With God's extravagant love made manifest in Jesus Christ at the centre of all we are and do, we will be able to endure our High Holy Days, Gethsemanes, betrayals, trials, suffering, and even death – and through even that right into the Source of Love itself in whom 'there is no darkness at all' (1 John 1:5). The setting of Mark's story suggests we might experience all this in the unlikeliest of places: in company with the poor, the afflicted, the lepers, the uncomprehending, and, well, women who lovingly squander their resources on others.

Prayer

*Lord Jesus, I pause at the midpoint of Holy Week
to thank you for the unlikely people
who provided its consolations for you.
Encourage me by their wisdom and goodness
to walk the whole way of the cross with you.
Remind me that parsimoniously 'counting the cost'
can deform and make the soul mingy and miserly.
Help me to see differently and to act gently,
to defend the unjustly accused and misunderstood.
May I see shining through this good material world,
the beauty of the spiritual.
In the midst of life's darkness and difficulties,
give me courage and let me be consolation for those around me.
Strengthen me to make of my life
an extravagant gift of love to you and to others,
knowing I can only do so
by the power of your death and resurrection.
Amen*

Maundy Thursday
In the shadows

Elaine Gisbourne

Bible reading: Matthew 26:69–75 (NIV)

Now Peter was sitting out in the courtyard, and a servant girl came to him. 'You also were with Jesus of Galilee,' she said.

But he denied it before them all. 'I don't know what you're talking about,' he said.

Then he went out to the gateway, where another servant girl saw him and said to the people there, 'This fellow was with Jesus of Nazareth.'

He denied it again, with an oath: 'I don't know the man!'

After a little while, those standing there went up to Peter and said, 'Surely you are one of them; your accent gives you away.'

Then he began to call down curses, and he swore to them, 'I don't know the man!'

Immediately a rooster crowed. Then Peter remembered the words Jesus had spoken: 'Before the rooster crows, you will disown me three times.' And he went outside and wept bitterly.

Reflection: In the shadows

We came across him one night, a young man, hunched on a pile of flattened cardboard boxes in the shadows between the cinema and Wetherspoon's, as late-night revellers passed him by. With his knees hugged to his chest, and his head buried in his arms, we were unsure if he could hear us, if he was even conscious. We greeted the top of his head; he didn't stir.

I sat next to him, as the others stood close by, three street pastors on duty on a damp January night. 'My name's Elaine, I don't think we've met,' my usual opening gambit. 'What's your name?'

He turned his head towards me, revealing half his face and a powerful smell of alcohol, the flat expression in his eye speaking of indifference to my presence and a loss of himself somewhere deep and distant. Without a word he turned away.

'Have you eaten today? We can get you some food, or a hot drink?' Our bags were stuffed with thick socks and gloves, bottles of water, first-aid supplies, sick-bags and flip-flops, but I sensed he wanted nothing from us, except to be left alone. I changed tack, 'Are you new to Lancaster? I've not seen you around before.'

'Don't be nice to me.' He spat the words, fixing me with a fierce glare. I rested my hand on his arm and waited.

'Tell me your name,' I tried again.

'JP, like the Pope, John Paul – you won't forget that.'

I smiled at him, 'Hello, JP, do you fancy a coffee?'

'I don't want anything; I don't deserve anything – give it to someone else who hasn't been drinking,' he said, just as a large, noisy crowd of young men dressed as superheroes came by, laughing and throwing banter at us as they passed.

'And exactly where round here might we find someone who hasn't been drinking?' I asked. JP caught my eye and half-smiled.

'So, JP, what brings you out on a night like this?' And gradually he laid out his story and his soul.

JP's mum and dad had never been together, and he hadn't got on with his mum. At the age of 15 she 'kicked him out' and he went to live with his dad; he hadn't seen his mum since.

JP's dad was 'not an easy man to live with', but their shared love of alcohol enabled them to get along together: JP soon became the alcoholic son of an alcoholic dad.

Then JP's dad died, and the young man was alone. Social services stepped in, and JP was allocated a social worker. They found him somewhere to live and, with their help and support, he was able to give up drinking, and felt valued for the first time in his life. He started a college course, was making friends and felt his life was turning round.

'Two days ago my social worker died,' JP said. 'I don't know why he died but I've got no one now. I don't know what to do, I can't cope. I went a bit crazy, and I had a drink. The place where I was living said I can't stay if I'm drinking, and kicked me out. I don't blame them: they've got the others there to think about. But the worst is, I've let them all down: my social worker, my dad. They tried to help me and I've let them down.' ...

'I'm still drinking,' JP said, 'I can't let you help me: I'll only let you down too.'

We sat together in silence for a while, in the stinking shadows, on soggy cardboard.

'Will you let me pray with you?' I ventured, unsure how JP would take this. But he looked at me in wonder, a faint light in his eye.

'Will you, really? No one's ever done that! Yes, please.'

So there we prayed: for JP's social worker and for his dad, and that JP would find peace and somehow know that he is loved.

Thursday night

The man edged closer to the glowing brazier,
but the hiss and spit of a girl's accusation
sent him scuttling back
into the dark.

Whispers chased and caught him,
and the black fear in his belly
spewed from his mouth
in a filth of lies.

But his poisonous words betrayed him,
and the whispers turned to shouts;
he rained loud curses on himself,
like stones.

The stars dissolved as the sky paled to grey,
and a cock-cry woke
the memory
of his loved one's words.

With bitter-salt self-loathing
he ran,
out into the cold.

Alone with his misery,
he hid
in the stinking shadows.

Prayer

Lord, beloved, we lose our way;
again and again we let you down,
with our words, our lies, our fear.
We betray your love,
and stain your image in us.

Lord, beloved, often we find ourselves
out in the dark night,
where deep shadows overwhelm us,
whispers taunt our minds,
where we feel far from your love for us.

Lord, beloved, we get afraid,
and we betray you;
we feel ashamed,
and we reject you;
we despair,
and we shun you.

Lord, beloved, when we are lost, come to us;
when we are afraid, strengthen us;
when we despair, reach out to us with your love,
and your words which say,

'Do not be afraid: you are mine.
You are my friend
and I love you.
Forgive yourself
as I forgive you.'
Amen

For a poem by Elaine Gisbourne about her work as a street pastor, go to 'Night sight' in the Resource section, p.129.

Good Friday
The veil of the temple

Stephen Wright

Reflection: The veil of the temple

Before reading this reflection you might like to listen to John Taverner's Veil of the Temple *(available on YouTube).*

As I write, I am listening to Taverner's magisterial *Veil of the Temple*. The music provides a perfect backdrop to a contemplation on Good Friday and prompts me into a childhood reminiscence.

The church was open and in darkness, all ornamentation and flowers removed; the cross shrouded with a white linen cloth. I asked my mum, 'Why is it called Good Friday if Jesus had been beaten and nailed to a cross?' My mum said, 'I don't know. I've never really thought about that.' And she just sat down in a pew and went very quiet. I fidgeted and thought about hot-cross buns to eat.

When we think of the brutality inflicted upon Jesus that day, 'good' does indeed seem to be a misnomer for this Friday. Yet the words 'God' and 'good' have the same Teutonic roots. Good Friday was God's day when something very powerful was happening beneath the surface impressions of horror. It is, paradoxically, a day of hope. Jesus, hitherto only available to those who met him, is about to undergo a transformation into the Christ consciousness to be available to all, unlimited by time and space.

I wonder if Jesus knew this. Only 24 hours before he had knelt in the Garden of Gethsemane in terrified prayer, so terrified that he sweat blood (a rare physiological phenomenon that can occur in conditions of extreme fear), and asked God if it wasn't possible for him to avoid his fate.

And he was withdrawn from them about a stone's cast, and kneeled down, and prayed, saying, 'Father, if you be willing,

> *remove this cup from me: nevertheless not my will, but yours, be done.' And there appeared an angel unto him from heaven, strengthening him. And being in agony he prayed more earnestly: and his sweat was as it were great drops of blood falling down to the ground* (Lk 22:41–44, KJB).

Was that 'angel' a deep inner knowing that he must trust God and that somehow he would pass through death? It is the classic 'Hero's journey' so eloquently described in Joseph Campbell's *The Hero with a Thousand Faces*. In order to transform and fulfil their quest, to become fully who he/she is, the hero/leader must die unto him/herself. Such a story is found in all traditions and is the archetype of modern stories – Gandalf, Aslan, Obi-Wan Kenobi – all die, must descend into darkness, before they can fulfil their destiny.

Perhaps that 'angel' gave Jesus the one thing he needed – hope. Enabling him to hand over in trust to God – *'not my will but Thine'*. These words are on my mother's grave and have been a meditation mantra for me down many a long year. One of the themes that the spiritual seeker encounters in both New and Old Age thinking is that fear must be overcome. Jesus encourages me. If he can be scared, even he – such a mighty and illumined being – then how much more so is it OK for me to feel fear and let it be. Jesus thus normalises fear, makes it OK to be human and weak.

Thus in the darkest of days, we see Jesus fall into despair in his agony on the cross:

> *Now from the sixth hour there was darkness over all the land unto the ninth hour. And about the ninth hour Jesus cried with a loud voice, saying, 'Eli, Eli, lama sabachthani?' That is to say, 'My God, my God, why hast thou forsaken me?'* (Matt 27:45–46, KJB).

These words echo Psalm 22:1. In his delirium Jesus was repeating lines he had heard and prayed many times before.

But he had also prayed and known that *'if I make my bed in hell, behold, thou art there'* (Ps 139:8). And *'Yea, though I walk through the valley of the shadow of death, I will fear no evil: for you are with me; your rod and staff they comfort me'* (Ps 23:4).

With this hope and trust, Jesus makes the ultimate surrender into God.

Then we see a transformation, and something very powerful happens:

> *And it was about the sixth hour, and there was a darkness over all the earth until the ninth hour. And the sun was darkened, and the veil of the temple was rent in the midst. And when Jesus had cried with a loud voice, he said, 'Father, into thy hands I commend my spirit': and having said thus, he gave up the ghost.* (Lk 23:44–46, KJB)

Perhaps it was here that Jesus came to know the 'darkness of God' – not as the darkness of evil, but of the mystery. The darkness of which the mystics speak that is illumined with its own impenetrable light-that-is-not-light. It is here where we are changed *'at the last trumpet'*.

But there is another great mystery, often overlooked, and which is sometimes interpreted as a sign of God's wrath and disapproval with the Jewish faith: the great storm tears up the temple curtain.

This curtain, of finest white linen with a blue, purple and scarlet pattern, protected the 'inner temple' in Jerusalem, the 'Holy of holies' where God's presence, the Presence, was said to be, and which could only be accessed by the High Priest once a year.

One day a few years ago when I was on Iona and in the Abbey church, I wandered down from the nave to the altar. Someone had left a Bible resting on that glorious great slab of white marble, veined with serpentine. It happened to be open at the story of the Crucifixion and my eyes were drawn to the passage about the curtain of the temple being torn. And there I was, in the temple, with no curtain separating me from the altar. The Abbey church is one of the few Christian places I visit regularly where there is no rail or barrier between people and altar. It is open, inviting, welcoming … Jesus' death and transformation through death opened an uncluttered Way to the Divine. The tearing of the veil is symbolic of a new relationship for all in God. Jesus' death removed any separation from God and the people of God.

Jesus' decent into Sheol is therefore full of paradox, for only by descending is he elevated, transformed from a bodily presence trapped by time and space into an eternal presence available to all.

It is often said that Iona as a place where the veil between realities is thinnest. Perhaps the reality is that there is really no veil at all. Jesus set us free from that. Such a belief in non-duality, non-separation is at the heart of the Iona Community's values, for just as we reject any barriers between God and the people of God, we reject any veils that create barriers between people.

The veil

You stand there still, beckoning, 'This Way!'
A way where there is no curtain any more.
Torn by death, obstruction is obliterated;
subverted by sacrifice, sabotaged by surrender.

The altar is approachable, proletarianised.
The Presence made accessible by profound humility.
The Holy of holies is everywhere,
the landscape is borderless,
no customs and excise, no patrols, no watchtowers;
no rail, no barrier to the forward step
and the planned inexorable return Home.

The veil of the temple, torn asunder.
Love broke in, completing her ineluctable destiny.

Not for nothing did You live.
Not for nothing did the thunder break and the sky darken.
Not for nothing did the wind tear at the sacred bells and the white linen.

Naked of time and space,
You are everywhere present, potent and unmasked.
You stretched Your bloodied arms on the cross and said,
'Here I am, see me.'
Opened arms, welcoming arms. Embracing. Greeting.
You set us free.
You stand there still, beckoning, 'This Way!'

Meditation and prayer

On Good Friday, and on other Fridays as well, I sometimes participate in a group called the 'Community of the three hours', which is given to prayerful contemplation from noon to 3pm, to remember the three hours that Jesus hung on the Cross.

Suggestion: this Good Friday keep a time of silence and stillness. During it pray:

> *Beloved God ... help me to be with Jesus in his time of suffering,*
> *and to know that in my times of suffering*
> *the light shines in the darkness.*
>
> *Help me to be open to that light.*
> *Help me to see in that light*
> *where I keep veils between myself and others,*
> *between myself and You,*
> *and between those parts of myself*
> *that are not healed and whole.*
>
> *Help me to strip away the veils of separation*
> *so that I may see You in all things and myself.*
> *In Jesus' name.*
> *Amen*

Holy Saturday
In our 'not there yet' world

Marie Pattison

Bible reading: Matthew 27:57–61, John 21:15–17 (NRSV)

When it was evening, there came a rich man from Arimathea, named Joseph, who was also a disciple of Jesus. He went to Pilate and asked for the body of Jesus; then Pilate ordered it to be given to him. So Joseph took the body and wrapped it in a clean linen cloth and laid it in his own new tomb, which he had hewn in the rock. He then rolled a great stone to the door of the tomb and went away. Mary Magdalene and the other Mary were there, sitting opposite the tomb …

When they had finished breakfast, Jesus said to Simon Peter, 'Simon son of John, do you love me more than these?' He said to him, 'Yes, Lord; you know that I love you.' Jesus said to him, 'Feed my lambs.' A second time he said to him, 'Simon son of John, do you love me?' He said to him, 'Yes, Lord; you know that I love you.' Jesus said to him, 'Tend my sheep.' He said to him the third time, 'Simon son of John, do you love me?' Peter felt hurt because he said to him the third time, 'Do you love me?' And he said to him, 'Lord, you know everything; you know that I love you.' Jesus said to him, 'Feed my sheep.'

Reflection: In our 'not there yet' world

I have never known the hunger that comes from having no money to buy food. I have known the hunger that comes from forgetting a packed lunch, being too busy, or from being too ill to eat, but I have never known the hunger that comes from an empty cupboard and an empty purse. Money was not plentiful when I was growing up – my parents did not own a car, our home did not have central heating – but food was plentiful. My mother would say 'the body needs food and the soul needs books' and I wanted for neither.

As an activist with Church Action on Poverty (www.church-poverty.org.uk) I know that many children are growing up in homes where food is scarce. Recently I watched the film *I, Daniel Blake*, by Ken Loach. In it a young mum who had gone without food to feed her children opens a can of beans she is given at a food bank and begins eating them with her hands. As she broke down in tears I struggled not to cry with her. I also know that her experience is real: 1 in 6 parents in this country goes hungry to feed their children. I think about that. I think about how hunger feels – that shaky wobbly level of tiredness where small tasks become difficult. And I think about being like that for days; worrying about small children, the benefits system, looking for a job, housing … My heart aches and I hunger for justice for everyone who has to experience injustice. I also know I am part of the problem: the price of the cappuccino I bought this morning, too rushed to make my own coffee, would make a huge difference to one of those parents, but I spend it unthinkingly. The problems can seem too big to tackle; where do I even start?

Maybe it is in today that we find our hope. Holy Saturday. A day that gets lost between the solemn grief of Good Friday and Sunday's celebration joy. I think of that first Holy Saturday. I think about Mary Magdalene's grief and despair, her day of living with it. Her friend cruelly executed and his dreams of a new

Kingdom seemingly in tatters. I think of the disciples, defeated, going back to their trade and having no success at that. It's important not to rush to the end; we know the end but the first disciples did not. They thought they had to live with their hopes and dreams of his Kingdom, another way of being, in ruins. And then this breakfast. Those who love Jesus are told what they must do with their love: 'Feed my sheep.'

We who know the end, who believe in good news and resurrection joy, also have to live in the 'not yet'. The Kingdom of justice and peace is not here, but we build it every time we speak up for justice, every time we feed someone, every time we change systems so people are not hungry. We bring some of this resurrection breakfast to life in our 'not there yet' world.

I know that I am called to listen to those who have an experience of hunger that I have never known. It would be easier not to; to put some cans in the church's food bank drop-off and tell myself I am doing enough. But to really listen, to hear the experience of a mother who can't provide for her children, is to need to change the system that allows that to happen. The dream of the Kingdom is a dream of the hungry fed, the humble lifted high. If we raise our voices – together we can end hunger in this country.

Prayer

Help me to see you, Jesus,
in every Good Friday:
asleep in the doorway of a shop,
signing on at the Job Centre,
queuing at the food bank.
Help me to see your suffering,
to wait at the foot of the cross.

Help me to see you, Jesus,
in moments of Sunday joy:
breakfast for the hungry,
the kindness of strangers,
justice for the oppressed.
Help me to see the signs
of your Kingdom breaking in.

Help me to love you, Jesus,
in this ordinary day:
not in helplessness at Friday's sorrow
or wrapped up in Sunday's joy.
But in the everyday Saturday world.
Help me to build your Kingdom.
Send me to feed your sheep.

Easter Sunday
God rolls away the stones

John McCall

**Bible reading: Matthew 28:1–10
(New Jerusalem Bible)**

After the Sabbath, and towards dawn on the first day of the week, Mary of Magdala and the other Mary went to visit the sepulchre. And suddenly there was a violent earthquake, for an angel of the Lord, descending from heaven, came and rolled away the stone and sat on it. His face was like lightning, his robe white as snow. The guards were so shaken by fear of him that they were like dead men. But the angel spoke; and he said to the women, 'There is no need for you to be afraid. I know you are looking for Jesus, who was crucified. He is not here, for he has risen, as he said he would. Come and see the place where he lay, then go quickly and tell his disciples, "He has risen from the dead and now he is going ahead of you to Galilee; that is where you will see him." Look! I have told you.' Filled with awe and great joy the women came quickly away from the tomb and ran to tell his disciples. And suddenly, coming to meet them, was Jesus. 'Greetings,' he said. And the women came up to him and, clasping his feet, they did him homage. Then Jesus said to them, 'Do not be afraid; go and tell my brothers that they must leave for Galilee; there they will see me.'

Reflection: God rolls away the stones

When we think of Easter worship, we may think of the sounds of brass and timpani and choirs singing ancient and new songs of the Resurrection. After the quieter tones of Passion Week – Easter is full of joy. But there is also a dimension of Easter which is quiet, reflective and full of mystery.

Last year I experienced a quiet Easter worship, perhaps much like that first Easter at Jesus' empty tomb. The Sign Language Church in Taipei, Taiwan asked me if I would preach at their Easter service. Their pastor, Pastor Wu, is a former student of mine. His wife and son can both hear, but they communicate as a family with sign language.

On that first Easter, Jesus rose in silence. No one witnessed the most important event in the history of the world. There were witnesses at the cross and at the Ascension, but there were no witnesses to Jesus' rising from the dead. And so, as I worshipped at the Sign Language Church, all the hymns and prayers and scripture were communicated in the silence of Mandarin sign language. I preached out loud in Mandarin and the pastor's wife translated into sign language. Some of the children and young adults can hear, but everyone can use sign language. Even though it was quiet, the responses on the faces of the worshippers were animated with Easter joy.

I talked about the fear of that first Easter, and how God rolls away the stones of fear in our lives. Fear blocks good news. Stones prevent us from living into Easter hope. The sign for 'do not fear' is two hands pushing out and two fingers on the palm of the hand shaking, like two legs of a person shaking. An apt symbol for the Easter text where the guards at the tomb shake and become 'like dead men'.

It made me think of an Easter here several years ago, when on Easter afternoon I was at the domestic airport checking in for a flight to the south, and we had a big earthquake. The ceiling tiles began to fall and we all ran outside, leaving our documents at the check-in counter. As we stood in front of the airport waiting for the ground to stop shaking, a reporter, without my knowing it, took a picture of us. The next day we were all on the front page of a local paper looking up at the swaying street lights. It was the first Easter when I really identified with those shaking guards.

It is not easy for deaf folk to believe in something that they cannot see. So Pastor Wu and his wife are currently translating their Bible into sign language, filming the signing and putting it on the Internet. They radiate joy as they seek, each day, to share Easter good news with the deaf folk of Taipei.

The other day Pastor Wu was talking to me about his eight years at the seminary. His wife translated every class lecture for him during those eight years. The seminary later gave her an honorary degree. Pastor Wu used to tell his classmates who slept through class, 'Please give me your ears – I really want to know what the professor is saying.'

It was a joy to see the fruit of this couple's labour as deaf folk of all ages participated in the Easter story. The sanctuary was quiet, but hearts were full of the good news of the Resurrection. In a culture where deaf folk are often marginalised, it was wonderful to see these deaf worshippers know that they are also included in the promise of an Easter life, both today and forever.

May the joy of Easter fill your days and may the stones which separate us from God and from each other in a fearful world be pushed aside as we witness to the wonder of this amazing promise.

Prayer

We rejoice, O God, that Jesus is risen!
We thank you and praise you on this Easter Day.
So fill us with the hope and promise of Easter,
that we may be your witnesses in our families,
our places of work
and in our communities.
In an increasingly fearful world
allow our churches to be agents of reconciliation and peace.
In the name of our resurrected Lord Jesus.
Amen

For another reflection by John McCall about his church and mission work in Asia, go to 'Invisible guests' in the Resources section, p.131.

Resources
for Holy Week

Prayers for the journey to Easter
(from Maundy Thursday to Easter Sunday)

'Chew on this': A prayer for Maundy Thursday

'Do this,
remember this,
chew on this,' he said.

Her hair is still fragrant with the oil
she poured on his feet,
just a few days ago;
now he kneels,
and pours water on hers.

'Do this,
remember this,
chew on this.'

The friends who were there
when he had thrown-over the tables
are now themselves thrown into disarray,
as his accusation causes them to doubt themselves,
and distrust each other.

'Do this,
remember this,
chew on this.'

The bread tastes fresh and familiar,
as fresh and familiar

as their often-recalled stories and adventures –
withered figs, angry Pharisees, raised daughters, satiated crowds …
but the feasting stops when he says,

'Do this,
remember this,
chew on this.'

And the plentiful wine,
wine of joy,
of weddings, of homecomings,
is now as precious and costly
as life itself, his life.

'Do this,
remember this,
chew on this.'

Lord, you throw us into disarray, just when we thought we knew you.
You confuse us, making what was simple and plain mysterious.
You, who brought life and healing to so many, tell us we must suffer.
You, who restored the outcast, say we must follow you
outside the city, outside society.

When we cannot understand, help us to trust you.
When we doubt ourselves, help us to know you.
When our lives are shaken, and our tables turned, help us to hold on to you.
When there are no answers, only confusion,
and the shadows threaten to overwhelm,
may we hear your words:

'Do this,
and remember me.'

'I thirst': A prayer for Good Friday

Hot, dry air burns his parched mouth and throat
with every laboured breath.
Cracked lips barely move,
scarcely enough breath to make the words audible,
'I thirst',
for an end to this.

Hot desert winds
lift the dust of the cracked, parched earth.
The Living Water is dry,
and dying.

The Living Water
is dry and dying,
and we struggle to watch, to stay.
We want to run from here,
or raise our fists and fight.

Give us the courage to still our feet,
to lower our fists,
and stay with you,
where you already are,
in the places where you suffer still.

Cloak us: A prayer for Holy Saturday

The birds are dumb,
and the dancing light on the tips of the waves is dull.
The wine vessels are drained dry,
and ashes lie heavy in the fireplace.
He lies entombed,
cold flesh on cold stone,
still body in still air,
silent now.

The one we flocked to,
who was so full of life that life itself sprung from him,
who was honoured by kings and widows,
is dead.

The one whose words stilled the storm,
called small men down from trees,
and elevated alienated women,
is silent.

The one whose passion, and compassion,
sharp wit and mischievous humour,
cut straight into our souls, and still loved us,
is cold.

And we, where are we now?
After the confusion and the shouting,
the horror of events unfolding,
after we stood, and watched him die;
we hide now in dark corners,

cradling our thoughts, our grief
and defeated hope.

O God, the light is gone,
and we are numb.
Cloak us in darkness, where we can hide for a while,
to mourn, to remember, and in time to cry.
Cloak us in your kindness, for as long as we need to stay.
And do not leave us.
Keep us safe.

Breadcrumbs: A prayer for Easter Sunday

The breadcrumbs are still falling from the loaf he held aloft
when realisation bursts in –
like the midday sun through thrown-back shutters.
'Chew on this,' he says. 'Remember.'

'Follow me,' he says, and the humour in his voice resonates with
the joy of living in the freedom beyond fear,
of living and loving beyond his dying bravely borne.
'Follow me,' he says, 'on this adventure into life.'

'Feast on me,' he says, 'for I love you and we are one.'
Bodies entwined, inseparable, even through death.
'Love one another,' he says, 'as I love you.'
Joyfully, completely, eternally!

'Celebrate with me now,' he says, 'for you are my friends,
with this wine of joy, costly and hard-won, shared with you whom I love.'
'This wine is for you,' he says, 'to sustain you:
for there are times when life feels too hard,
and you will need to remember.'

In the nourishing bread,
in the overflowing cup,
in the love beyond measure,
in the life beyond suffering,
in the joy beyond fear,
in each dawn after dark night,
'Remember me.'

Elaine Gisbourne

Crucifixion 2017-style

We have a law
and by that law he ought to be
in work.
He isn't?
It's his fault.
He ought to be punished, have a lower
income,
have no income,
ought to be hungry,
thirsty,
in debt,
in prison,
live in a flat with only
one bedroom,
pay extra rent for a
spare bedroom,
be homeless,
meet the bailiffs;
he ought to be stressed
to breaking point.

She ought not to have had
a large family with
high benefit income.
It is not fair
on rich people
that some women and children
are poor.

It is better for the rest of us
that poor people

die young.

Paul Nicolson, Taxpayers Against Poverty

My love is like a red, red rose

Strong in strange soils she roots deep
under many strange suns she draws life
no great mischief her petals have fallen
in many strange lands

her thorns are stained blood red
blood of my daughters and my sons
she bled in Basra and Tiananmen
Wounded Knee and Jenin
Hiroshima and My Lai
Glencoe and Chechnya
in Belsen they burned her to ashes
with Martin Luther King
and a million voices she sang hope
in Birmingham, Alabama and Washington
she was beaten and gassed in Seattle
in Genoa they shot her dead with Carlo Giuliani
she was hanged on Glasgow Green
with the Radical Martyrs

today she begs for bread in Haiti
and cries for water in Angola
in Gaza she weeps by her ruined home
in Bangkok her daughters work
rich tourists, her sons their pimps

so many times with tanks and guns
they have crushed her petals
yet still each day she blooms red
fresh and clear as morning birdsong
she greets the sun with hope
and gentle defiance unyielding

Rosa mundi, Rosa mystica
within and without one love
her touch in a stranger's hand
a stranger's smile her bloom
her scent in my children's hair
her warmth in my lover's kiss

long ago
my father planted her in a garden
my mother tended her with patience and prayer
I buried them both and know
all this earth is my father's grave
all her children are one

sacred the soil
red the rose
this red, red rose
my love.

Brian Quail

'This is my child'

In memory of three-year-old Aylan Kurdi and so many others ...

'This is my child.'

We feel the mother's loss
As, weeping and forlorn,
She gazes at the cross.
'This is my child.'

As, smashed on any road,
Or washed up on a shore,
She sees her precious load.
'This is my child.'

He paid the price of sin,
Our wanton love of speed,
Of power, our lust to win.
'This is my child.'

You turn and walk away.
The mother cannot leave.
Where she goes, he will stay.
'This is my child.'

And how then can he rise?
Unless we open wide
Our arms, our hearts, our eyes.
'This is my child.'

And he will have no hope
Unless we dare to look
At broken life
On shore, on road.
Until with mothers we proclaim:
'This is my body and my blood.'

Anna Briggs

'May peace prevail'
An interview with Lyn Ma, Neil Squires

> *In May 2016, Lyn Ma, who teaches ESOL at Glasgow Clyde College, organised a residential trip to Allanton World Peace Sanctuary (www.worldpeace-uk.org) for a group of unaccompanied asylum seekers and refugees. The trip was partly supported through the donations of members and associates of the Iona Community. Neil Squires, an Iona Community member and a close friend, asks Lyn about her work and the trip ...*

Neil: Why does Glasgow Clyde College have such a high number of young asylum seekers and refugees?

Lyn: Adult asylum seekers and refugees began to be dispersed to Glasgow over 10 years ago, as a result of Glasgow City Council signing a housing and support services agreement with the Home Office. It still has the highest number of asylum seekers/refugees in Scotland. It became apparent that young people between the ages of 16-20 were also being dispersed, usually without family but not always. Glasgow Clyde College responded by creating a more age-appropriate and holistic course that includes art, drama and music as well as outdoor learning and personal and social development. This 16+ ESOL (English for Speakers of Other Languages) programme is unique in Scotland.

Neil: Where are the young people from?

Lyn: They come from a variety of countries; initially many young people came from Somalia, Afghanistan and were also Iraqi Kurds. This demographic has changed and countries that young people come from now include Guinea, Ivory Coast, Albania, Congo, Eritrea, Georgia, Sudan, Syria, Iran, Iraq, and most recently many young people who have been trafficked from China and Vietnam. They are predominantly young men as it is much more difficult for young women to escape.

Neil: What has happened to them and what kinds of issues are they living with?

Lyn: Many young people are fleeing civil war or unrest but some of them have families that have worked for the British Government in countries like Afghanistan and Iraq and have been targeted by the Taliban, who have threatened them and their families. Other young people have been escaping forced military service. Some young people have been persecuted and tortured because of their sexuality or religious beliefs. Other young people have been trafficked for sexual exploitation and domestic servitude in cannabis farms or nail bars. Many of these young people have not been educated or have experienced a fractured education; they are often suffering from multiple levels of grief, trauma and loss. They are mostly alone without any family or friends in an unknown country, having often endured horrendous and dangerous journeys to get to Scotland, and are unsure of what the future holds for them.

Neil: What is your role at Glasgow Clyde College and how long have you been there?

Lyn: I have been at Glasgow College, a large further education college, for over 10 years. I am a Senior Lecturer in ESOL and among other things that I do, I have responsibility for running the 16+ ESOL programme. Referrals for the course come from social work departments, schools, the British Red Cross and many other agencies. I test the English language level of the young people and they start college, if there are places available. I also teach the young people and have overall responsibility for their guidance and wellbeing.

Neil: How did the idea for a residential trip come about and what is the Allanton Centre?

Lyn: As someone who worked as a programme worker on Iona and a year-long volunteer at Corrymeela when I was in my 20s, I have seen the amazing difference a residential experience can make to young people. For this group of young people, it is the only opportunity to experience something that is most like 'family'. They thoroughly enjoy eating and sharing with each other. For most of them they have lived communally and the loss of family and friends is devastating. For this one weekend they can be like other young people and have fun but also share with each other in a completely different way from being in a classroom. Our links with Allanton Peace Sanctuary began several years ago. It is a big old house in Dumfries, with beautiful gardens and grounds and is a place dedicated to building world peace. Like the MacLeod Centre on Iona, accommodation is shared dorms and all meals are eaten together.

Neil: Tell me about this year's trip.

Lyn: This year 15 young people went to Allanton. They were all between the ages of 16-19 and they had studied together in my class over the last academic year. The focus of the weekend was providing the young people with opportunities to share together practical activities like gardening, playing on the beach, writing songs, singing and dancing round the bonfire. As well as that, we shared reflection times together in the peace room, where young people had the chance to voice their hopes and dreams for their lives and to hear others say positive things about them and their individual gifts and talents. A unique part of the Allanton experience is the flag ceremony, where every country's flag is held aloft and we all say together, 'May peace prevail' in the country of each flag. This is always very moving as the young people hold their own flags and we all wish and pray for peace.

Neil: What were the other highlights of the trip?

Lyn: We saw young people smiling, laughing, building deeper relationships with each other that will help sustain them in the difficult times ahead. One of the most wonderful things we heard over and over again was, 'This is the best weekend of my life', 'I never thought I could have friends like this' and 'This is the first time since I left my country I have felt part of a family.' For young people who feel so alone and lost just being together is so valuable and profound.

Neil: How did the Iona Community help?

Lyn: Every year we need to raise money to make this residential happen. It is not a huge amount of money – £2000 – but it is not part of the college budget and so the money needs to be raised from elsewhere. Obviously the young people do not have the money to pay for themselves. This year members of the Iona Community both individually and in Family Groups very generously raised enough money that allowed us to make this happen. As well as the money donated, I was so touched by the warm messages of support that Iona Community members and associates sent to me and to the young people.

Neil: What else can the Iona Community do?

Lyn: That is a difficult question … there are so many ways in which members, associates and friends can help these young people. By supporting any campaigns to put pressure on the Westminster Government to bring more unaccompanied minors to the UK to be reunited with family or looked after by others. Also to protest to your MP at the unjust and inhumane immigration laws that allow young people over 18 to be detained or refused asylum and denied the chance to be educated and live in safety in the UK.

Neil: Thank you for the inspirational work that you do, for sharing the moving experiences of your trip to Allanton, and for the suggestions of how we might further support the needs of young asylum seekers and refugees.

Lyn Ma and Neil Squires

You – yes – you
A meditation on Simon of Cyrene

Jesus falls for the third time. You are watching. You hear the crack of the whips, the cursing and spitting of the soldiers. You are frozen in disbelief, as if caught in time.

'You – yes, you – you!'

Suddenly your arm is grabbed roughly and you are dragged from the crowd. 'You – yes, you – you!' They push the prisoner roughly aside with the scourge and between them they drag the cross onto your back. You have no time to draw breath, to think, to question. It is your cross now – rough-hewn, splinters digging into your skin, a graze on your cheek already smarting. You hear the whip crack before you feel it. You stagger and begin to walk. You steady yourself, sway a little and then, finding a kind of balance, you take another step. The cross is heavy, heavier than anything you've carried before. Heavier than the boats, laden with fish, that you drag so easily onto the shore. Those boats are full of life and surrounded by the happy yet hungry. Here, the last meal has already been eaten ... not yours, but his. 'You – yes, you – you!' ...

Sometimes we do not have the luxury of thought, prayer, reflection. Sometimes it just happens, in a heart-stopping moment, that we are chosen for life and for death, out of the crowd, and we have no choice, no time to think and carefully weigh the options. The prisoner has fallen. His torturers have chosen you to help now. You – yes – you. In this action you are the helper of death and of life. You are compromised. You are the courageous one and the coward. Only after the cross is raised, and the soldiers have crucified him, is there a moment for you to pause and to pray.

Alison Swinfen

Prayers on crucifixion

It's easy to think of the Crucifixion as something that happened a long time ago. But for some people every day is Good Friday. People forced into poverty, those who are homeless. Those seeking asylum. People crushed by debt and treated with contempt by the powerful. Jesus is crucified today in their suffering ...

Asylum seekers:

Lord, it's so easy to think of asylum seekers
(when we think of them at all)
as Other.
As foreign.
Different in colour and perhaps religion.
We think of them as distant.
We are tempted to think of them coming to 'our' country.
Yes, there's distance and a feeling of separation in the idea of asylum.
But help us, Lord, to remember that,
at the hour of our own death,
we ourselves will be asylum seekers.
Hoping and praying for sanctuary
and a loving welcome with you in heaven.
Let our own mortality help us to be one
with those who seek asylum in Britain today.
And let us offer them gladly
the hospitality of love
that is your gift to us all.
Amen

Debt:

Why did we do it, Lord?
Rewrite your prayer.
You said cancel our debts,
but we preferred forgive us our trespasses.
Which sounds a lot more dignified.
Moderate. Respectable.
But you, it seems, said debts –
and you said it to people experiencing crushing debt.
Debt that brought dishonour, destitution and death.
We prefer the calm of organised religion,
but your focus was on organised greed and oppression.
Debt is still with us today – in spades.
Help us, Lord, to remember that debt and the struggle for justice
are at the heart of our spirituality.
And at the heart of Your Prayer.
Amen

Food banks:

OK, Lord, we've got it now.
Money banks are bad, food banks are good.
And, it has to be said,
food banks certainly help people: lots of hungry people.
They're a symbol of caring and compassion.
So, why didn't you set up food banks, Lord?
Or walk-in clinics, come to that?
There were vast numbers of hungry and sick people

in first-century Palestine.
It's only very gradually we realise
your miracles were a sign not a solution.
Your solution was an end to injustice and oppression.
But that threatened the system:
the system operated by the rich and powerful.
Looking back on all that,
it's clear that the Cross was inevitable.
But no one is likely to get crucified for running a food bank.
Which should make us think.
Maybe we need to go beyond the Good Samaritan, as you did.
Amen

The homeless:

Lord, there's a children's game of skimming flat pebbles across a lake:
watching them bounce along its surface.
Maybe you played the game as a child at the Sea of Galilee.
The trouble is, Lord,
we play that game with the Gospel.
We skim over it.
You said 'the son of man has nowhere to lay his head'.
We read those familiar words,
but we don't want to let them sink in.
We don't really take in the fact
that you were often homeless:
no shelter, no bed, no toilet paper.
You were alongside the homeless.
And they, in turn, gave you loyalty and love.

Today you meet us among the homeless.
And in that encounter,
we discover the depth of your love –
for them and for ourselves.
Amen

The living wage:

They were a great idea, Lord.
Your parables.
Simple stories with simple messages.
But it seems we still manage to get them wrong.
The labourers in the vineyard, for example.
Was that about a generous landowner?
An image of God himself?
Or was it about exploitation:
a rich man paying starvation wages to zero-hours labourers?
And then, on top of that,
setting them at each other's throats?
Was there a hard edge to your story?
One that the poor
and those turned off their land
would have recognised?
You came that we may have life.
All of us.
That means justice, respect
and a 'living' wage.
A life-giving wage.
In a world of plenty,

anything less than that is an injustice.
A denial of your promise.
God's promise.
Amen

Welfare and work:

Lord, why do so many people snigger
at the mention of health and safety?
Isn't that exactly what we wish for our loved ones?
We care about their well-being.
Their welfare.
That's what love means, isn't it?
So how is it that 'welfare' has become such a dirty word
in the tabloids and in the mouths of so many politicians?
An insult. A judgement.
An expression of sneering contempt.
But you were born into the world
because of the Father's concern for our welfare.
Our well-being.
Our shalom.

Lord, let us find useful, meaningful work as we can,
but let us always seek the welfare, the health and the safety,
of our neighbour.
Even of our politicians.
Amen

Child poverty:

Lord, it's amazing that many centuries ago we started
cutting and pasting the Gospel.
The bits we were uncomfortable with got deleted:
at least in our minds.
Like when you said
you came to bring good news to the poor.
But we deleted 'to the poor'
and inserted the words: to us.
You said the last shall be first.
But a church controlled by men
never asked who 'the last' actually were.
They were the women and the children:
the ones without power.
Maybe those at the foot of the cross.
So when we pray for an end to child poverty,
help us to remember, Lord,
that in those words we come very close to your love,
your pain –
and to your anger at injustice.
Amen

David Rhodes

Take us back

Good Friday worship on the words from the Cross

> *For this service the front of the worship space is left empty. All contributors are dispersed among the congregation and use radio mics. You will need seven voices.*

Introduction:

Voice 1: In this service there is no leader.

Voice 2: The disciples were without their leader that first Easter.

Voice 3: In this service there is a lot of silence

Voice 4: which some will find uncomfortable.

Voice 5: The first Easter was far from a comfortable experience.

Voice 6: In this service you are invited to listen and reflect,

Voice 7: to consider and pray …

Chant/song: 'Stay with me' (Taizé), or 'When the son of God was dying', by John L. Bell and Graham Maule, from *Enemy of Apathy: Songs and chants for Lent, Eastertide and Pentecost*, Wild Goose Publications (This song could instead be read out verse by verse by different voices.)

Voice 1: God we come before you.
So many years after that first Good Friday.
So many generations have come
and gone
since then.

Silence (about 15 seconds)

Voice 2: Take us back.
Back to the horror
and bewilderment of that day.
Not to glory in pain,
or to revel in murder.

Silence (about 15 seconds)

Voice 3: Take us back,
to bear witness to what you have done,
and to what you continue to do …

Silence (about 15 seconds)

Voice 4: Lord, we long for all injustice to end.
All sorrow and suffering to halt.
All pain and despair to be stopped.
Once and for all.

Silence (about 15 seconds)

Voice 5: Yet you choose to remain with us
in the mess of our lives,
in the unfinished tangle of our days.

Silence (about 15 seconds)

Voice 6: Take us back
to another time when darkness seemed to triumph,
when death appeared to have the upper hand.

Silence (about 15 seconds)

Voice 7: Take us back
to listen to what you said
when all hope appeared lost.

Silence (about 15 seconds)

Song: 'Were you there when they crucified my Lord?'

Sung solo: Were you there when they crucified my Lord?
Were you there when they crucified my Lord?
Oh, sometimes it causes me to tremble, tremble, tremble.
Were you there when they crucified my Lord?

Silence

Voice 1: 'Forgive them, Father. They don't know what they are doing.'

Silence

Solo: Were you there when he cried, 'Father, forgive'?

All: Were you there when he cried, 'Father, forgive'?
Oh, sometimes it causes me to tremble, tremble, tremble.
Were you there when they crucified my Lord?

Resources for Holy Week

       Silence

Voice 2:   'I promise that today you will be in Paradise with me.'

       Silence

Solo: Were you there when he welcomed home a thief?

All: Were you there when he welcomed home a thief?
Oh, sometimes it causes me to tremble, tremble, tremble.
Were you there when they crucified my Lord?

       Silence

Voice 3:   'Woman, here is your son … Here is your mother.'

       Silence

Solo: Were you there when his mother gained a son?

All: Were you there when his mother gained a son?
Oh, sometimes it causes me to tremble, tremble, tremble.
Were you there when they crucified my Lord?

       Silence

Voice 4:   'My God, my God, why have you forsaken me?'

       Silence

Solo: Were you there when he felt that God had gone?

All: Were you there when he felt that God had gone?

Oh, sometimes it causes me to tremble, tremble, tremble.
Were you there when they crucified my Lord?

Silence

Voice 5: 'I thirst.'

Silence

Solo: Were you there when he longed to slay his thirst?

All: Were you there when he longed to slay his thirst?
Oh, sometimes it causes me to tremble, tremble, tremble.
Were you there when they crucified my Lord?

Silence

Voice 6: 'It is finished.'

Silence

Solo: Were you there when he cried, 'Now it is done'?

All: Were you there when he cried, 'Now it is done'?
Oh, sometimes it causes me to tremble, tremble, tremble.
Were you there when they crucified my Lord?

Silence

Voice 7: 'Father, into your hands I commit my spirit.'

Silence

Solo: Were you there when he gave his life to God?

All:	Were you there when he gave his life to God? Oh, sometimes it causes me to tremble, tremble, tremble. Were you there when they crucified my Lord?

Longer silence

Voice 1: Take us back to that hellish confinement.

Silence (about 15 seconds)

Voice 2: Take us back to the point of despair.

Silence (about 15 seconds)

Voice 3: Take us back to the place of great darkness.

Silence (about 15 seconds)

Voice 4: Take us back from our own hellish confinement.

Silence (about 15 seconds)

Voice 5: Take us back from our own point of despair.

Silence (about 15 seconds)

Voice 6: Take us back from our own place of darkness.

Silence (about 15 seconds)

Voice 7: Take us back to our home in the heart of God.

Silence (about 30 seconds)

Voice 1: Today is not a day for exuberant celebration.

Silence (about 15 seconds)

Voice 2:   Today is not a day for airbrushing problems.

Silence (about 15 seconds)

Voice 3:   Today is not a day for joyful delusions.

Silence (about 15 seconds)

Voice 4:   Today is not that kind of day.

Silence (about 15 seconds)

Voice 5:   Today is a day for sorrowful sighing.

Silence (about 15 seconds)

Voice 6:   Today is a day for bewildered grieving.

Silence (about 15 seconds)

Voice 7:   Today is a day for placing our broken spirits in your hands.

Silence (about 15 seconds)

All: And so we place our broken spirits in your hands.

Chant: 'Behold the Lamb of God (1)', by John L. Bell, from *Come All You People*, Wild Goose Publications

Folk may remain in silence for as long as is helpful.

David McNeish

Your life in us
Prayers on the seven words from the Cross

'Forgive them, Father. They don't know what they are doing.'
Luke 23:34

Prayer

And Lord, we are the same
centuries later.
Day by day,
we act without wisdom,
without awareness,
without compassion.
Half the time
we simply don't know what we are doing
as we disconnect from your
enduring Light.
Today, may we be humble enough
to recognise our failures and to seek your help.
With our mind and with our heart.

'I promise you that today you will be in Paradise with me.'
Luke 23:43

Prayer

Thank you, Lord,
for this mind-blowing invitation
which you first offered to the thief hanging beside you

on that fateful day –
and today offer to us.
May we stop for a moment and
hear again this loving invitation,
embedded in God's grace,
which draws us close to the One
who understands us all.

'He is your son: she is your mother.'
John 19:26–27

Prayer

You hold the world in your hands,
yet know our human intimacies.
On the cross you thought of your mother and your friends.
You cared for their future.
And right where we are
that caring love enfolds us,
tenderly reminding us
that in the midst of ordinary living,
your Spirit is with us,
sometimes challenging,
always surprising.

'My God, my God, why did you abandon me?'
Mark 15:34

Prayer

We struggle, we fall,
we fail, we cry out
and often ask this question ourselves.
God help us in some small way to understand
that when we believe you are silent
or far off,
or have ditched us completely,
that there still remains a simple truth:
that we are not abandoned,
but held.

'I am thirsty.'
John 19:28

Prayer

Jesus, in your agony you asked for a drink.
And today
we know that you walk with all who hunger and thirst
in our divided world.
Help us to walk with them too,
taking risks for love,
being passionate for justice,
abandoning, even for a moment,
our endless need for comfort,
for security, for things.

'It is finished.'
John 19:30

Prayer

Lord, through this day may we experience
that inner strength which bears and believes and hopes
and endures all things.
For yours is the goodness
that makes sense of this day,
and brings calm to our souls.

'Father, into your hands I place my spirit.'
Luke 23:46

Prayer

We pause:
we are still:
we listen:
we hear;
we pause again:
we look around,
we move on –
refreshed
and ready again
to celebrate the miracle of life.
Your life in us.

Peter Millar

Holy Week poems

From *From Darkness to Eastering*

Tenebrae

Oblivious to the outside world,
we drop our lamentations
into utter darkness,
chant cries to Jerusalem,
calls to return,
sing haunted antiphons,
then kneel in silence.

Outside the church,
out beyond humanity's
long night watch,
a lone bird warbles.
Regardless of us,
in the selfless east,
the sun slowly rises.

The harrowing of Hell

'... mercy triumphs over judgement'
James 2:13

In the icons, Jesus
victoriously straddles
a gaping darkness,
firmly grasps
by their pale hands
Adam and Eve,
like the carnival
strongman who sounds
the bell with his blow,
exultantly pulls them
from shattered sepulchres.

But before all this
there must have been
a great assize, separation
of sheep from goats.
Hell was populated,
peopled with the judged
(like our ancient parents).
Prior justice carried out
in some cosmic courtroom,
was now completed
as mercy drew it,
blinking uncomprehendingly,
triumphantly forth
from darkness and death.

Dust to dust

Our life's pilgrimage
is unicursal.
There might be seasons
of long wandering,
or time traversing
a verdant valley,
rest by still waters,
a hard ascending
of forbidding heights,
or diversions down
dreadful dead ends.
Yet the path remains,
perhaps obscure, but
universally
one directional.
In the eternal
human procession
each one's journey winds
to a gaping grave.
Each person is a
one-way street toward
the matter from which
they were constructed,
the stuff underfoot
into which God breathed,
will again breathe, life.

First light

Easter feast's first light
occurs outside church,
a fire we build
in the parking lot,
carry with singing
into the nave's
obscure, dark cavern
soon awash with words
about mysteries which
are unspeakable.

Much later I stand
mute, awestruck beneath
'the moon and stars
which Thou hast made',
smell in spring's wet earth
Easter day's first light
silently creeping
over hill and field,
just as Christ's rising,
forever's first dawn,
blossoming outside
the church's confines.

Bonnie Thurston

We will tread the earth lightly
A service of lamentation to liberate us for action

Opening responses:

Before God, who loves us with great compassion,
We come with our sorrows.

For the damage to this planet,
We are weeping, Creator God.

For the unequal consequences for the poor,
We are weeping, shepherding God.

For the refugees fleeing war and injustice,
We are weeping, travelling God.

For children alone, abducted or astray,
We are weeping, Mothering God.

For the denials and fears within us,
We are weeping, Holy God.
Loving God,
take away the fears that freeze us
and give us the courage to live your compassionate justice.
Amen

Song: 'Christ be our light', by Bernadette Farrell, CH4 543

Introduction:

When it comes to addressing the environmental damage we are inflicting on the planet, many of us freeze, feeling powerless in the face of the enormity of it all, or deny the problem, or take a tiny action, hoping that it will do. The value of lamentation is that it can unfreeze us, and lead to action.

Lamenting, well-recognised in the Psalms, allows us to grieve together and offer our sorrows to God. Lamenting so often gets left out of our worship, but it is as powerful as praise, and necessary for our souls to grow.

So in this service we will lament together, and speak out our sorrow, trusting that God will lighten the path for change.

Lament and confession:

Kneel or sit.

Leader: We lament the damage done to God's world and the poverty of our international relationships. We offer our sorrow for forgiveness and healing.

A: Loving God, in Jesus you stepped up to the line, bit the bullet, owned the problem.

B: Walk beside us as we live with the evidence that the earth is under threat. Share our pain for the way we have avoided the truth and ignored the signs.

All: And free us from the guilt that binds us …

A: Loving God, in Jesus you laid yourself open, stuck your neck out and made yourself vulnerable to the whims of earthly rulers.

B: Walk beside us as we risk the consequences of challenge. Share our pain for what has been done in selfishness and blindness.

All: And free us from the guilt that binds us …

A: Loving God, in Jesus you grasped the nettle, picked up the shovel, became involved.

B: Walk beside us as we speak for justice and struggle with change. Share our pain for what has not been done through fear and weakness.

All: And free us from the guilt that binds us …

A: Loving God, in Jesus you faced the music, carried the can, took the blame.

B: Walk beside us as we own our human failure. Share our pain for what has been done in foolishness and ignorance.

All: And free us from the guilt that binds us …

Leader: The forgiveness of Jesus be yours; the strength of the Creator be yours; and the Spirit inspire your living.

All: Amen

Bible reading: Lamentations 5:1–10, 19–22

Reflection: The public voicing of pain

… People in pastoral ministry learn about the stages of grief: the shock, the denial, the anger, the deep sadness. In the West, perhaps we are somewhere between denial and anger. But the sadness will come, as it has for those who have either experienced or studied in depth the scale of what is happening.

Such immense sorrow can have a paralysing effect. The biblical tradition of lamentation – the public voicing of pain – is one important way in which people in huge crisis have responded and sought to find a way through their disempowerment. The Book of Lamentations, sitting firmly in the middle of the prophetic books of the Hebrew Bible, laments the fall of Jerusalem and the beginning of the Babylonian captivity. Its poems are still used today in Jewish liturgy. It has allowed people to name their loss, their complicity and their fear, to turn passive despair into active mourning and to release the energy trapped in maintaining denial into energy for action and change.

Lamentation has been an important aspect of all movements for justice, peace and freedom. In a culture which is terrified of failure, loss and grief, finding the appropriate spaces for lamentation is not easy, but I think it is essential. A sense of place, a profound love of a particular landscape, is a deep human instinct, even when that landscape does not appeal to everyone. In his moving and beautiful book *Palestinian Walks*, Raja Shehadeh describes a territory that has often been found bleak, barren and intimidating to visitors – with the eyes of love and a different way of seeing. It is a remembering of a place that is already disappearing through environmental degradation.

Many find the remote wilderness places of Scotland, the bare hills and strange rock formations, equally challenging. To me, they are beautiful beyond compare.

We need ways of remembering and naming, in sorrow and anger, what we have loved, even as it is under threat. To release these is also to release our power for repentance and change. Liturgy has always been a way of doing this, what Walter Brueggemann has called 'liturgical resistance' …

Time is running out fast. Now is time for anger and sorrow that liberates us for action.

Kathy Galloway, from A Heart for Creation

In groups of two or three, share your thoughts about the readings.

Song: 'God our Maker, hear our cry'
Tune: 'Aus der tiefe (Heinlein)'/'Forty days and forty nights'

God our Maker, hear our cry,
sorrow for our lack of care.
We have used your gifts for life
without thought and without prayer.

Gifts unfairly shared around,
though you gave enough for all.
We preferred to store up wealth;
fear and greed has us in thrall.

We regret our carbon use
now we know it hurts the earth;
caught in systems hard to change,
lead us on a wiser path.

Breathe forgiveness over us,
free our souls to pay the price,
serve creation day by day,
follow Christ in sacrifice.

Chris Polhill

A version of Psalm 10:

A: Why are you so far away, O God –
so elusive when we have greatest need of you?

B: Look how wicked people are oppressing the weak
by consuming scarce resources and causing disasters.

A: They flaunt their wealth to become famous,
having no regard for your Gospel.
They mock those who put their trust in you
and claim that life has no purpose.

B: They put their trust in wealth and power
and believe that they are in control.

A: Their lifestyle is one of self-seeking pleasure;
they have no regard for the damage they do.

B: They play on the weakness of others
to ensnare them in their own folly.

A: They accept no responsibility for the state of the world,
looking only for ways to protect themselves.

B: They think that their desires are paramount
and see no need to justify their actions.

A: We long to see them brought down,
for the oppressed to take power.
Why should these people be free to act selfishly
and think they will never face the consequences?

B: We believe that you share the misery and pain
of all the oppressed and exploited,
that you stand beside the weak
and are torn as creation suffers.

A: We want to end the power of evil,
to bring about your kingdom here.
Today, give us strength to name wrongful acts
and to listen to the cries of the poor.

B: Show us how to bring about fairer societies
where everyone has a chance.
So that no one goes in fear for themselves,
their loved ones, or the places they treasure.

Stations for prayer and reflection:

Give folk lots of time and space for this. People can visit one, two or all the stations.

Station 1: Lamenting the suffering of refugees and displaced people:

Use images from print media and the Internet. People are invited to write their feelings/a word(s) next to the different photos.

Station 2: Lamenting the greed that damages the planet:

Folk are invited to place a candle/tea-light next to the kind of greed they most want to lament:

Card 1: Fuel waste, with phrases such as: 'Using a car more than we need to', 'Not using public transport', 'Central heating turned up too high', 'Air travel' …

Card 2: Electronic and electric goods waste, with phrases such as: 'We replace rather than repair', 'Hard to recycle, so it ends up in the landfill', 'We are tempted to buy the latest models', 'How many unwanted electric and electronic goods do we own/how many unused gadgets in our homes?' …

Card 3: Textile and clothes waste, with current statistics about clothes and textile waste and the cost of cheap clothes to the planet and to the people who make them: see, for example, the Clean Clothes Campaign, etc.

Card 4: Food waste, with current statistics about food waste: search the Internet for information.

Station 3: Lamenting the decline in faith:

Folk are invited to sit and reflect on Bible verses, and then to light a candle. Suggested Bible verses (write these on big cards): 1 Kings 19:14, Isaiah 44:2, Jeremiah 5:1, Jeremiah 18:1, Matthew 24:37, Mark 6:5–6.

Gather everyone, then together say the Lord's Prayer.

Song: 'Don't be afraid', from *Come All You People,* John L. Bell, Wild Goose Publications

Leader: 'We need ways of remembering and naming, in sorrow and anger, what we have loved, even as it is under threat. To release these is also to release our power for repentance and change.' *(Kathy Galloway)*

Let us say our affirmation:

Affirmation:

With the whole church,
We affirm
that we are made in God's image,
befriended by Christ, empowered by the Spirit.

With people everywhere,
We affirm
God's goodness at the heart of humanity,
planted more deeply than all that is wrong.

With all creation,
**We celebrate
the miracle and wonder of life,
the unfolding purposes of God,
forever at work in ourselves and the world.**

(From *Iona Abbey Worship Book*)

Song: 'Christ be beside me, Christ be before me' (various songbooks)

Closing responses:

We will tread the earth lightly:
Scattering God's blessing.

Our hearts changed by love:
The love of the Living God.

Working to transform the world –
Inspired by the Holy God.

Sung blessing: 'God's eye be within me (God's foot be before me)', from *There Is One Among Us*, John L. Bell, Wild Goose Publications

Chris Polhill

Sources:

Prayers and other resources in this liturgy taken from *A Heart for Creation: Worship Resources and Reflections on the Environment*, Chris Polhill, Wild Goose Publications, 2010

The disturbing and good news
(Holy Saturday on Iona)

Holy Week on Iona was my first experience with Holy Saturday. It was a rather dreary, misty, *dreich* day. I remember gathering in the Chapter house for a session of 'Singing the blues', led by Wild Goose Resource Group worker Mairi Munro. After, it was a good day simply to wander around the island, to sit in the silence of the Abbey, and to try to absorb, perhaps for the first time in my life, the enormity, the meaning, the sense of that day. And what surprised me most was how often my thoughts turned to Judas, of all people.

Judas intrigues a lot of us. Was he simply a mercenary of money, stealing from the common purse, and willing to sell his teacher for a few bucks? Was he as callous towards the poor, the oppressed, the outcast as some of the Gospels portray? Was he the willing, or unwitting, pawn of the religious and political authorities of his day, or even of the Evil One?

I'm not sure; I can't figure him out. Yet, I know that in John's Gospel, he is there at the Last Supper, and that says something to me about Jesus' inclusive love. In fact, when Jesus dips the morsel of bread and hands it to Judas, this is a traditional way of honouring a person – and an interesting way to treat the person who is about to betray you!

Of course, I can't figure Judas out because I can't figure out my *own* relationship with Jesus.

After all, if Jesus is in the poor of the world, and I refuse to see them as sisters and brothers in Christ, what makes me different from Judas?

And if I think we should spend money on our own 'kind', whether they are in my church, my community, my country, before helping anyone else out, is my attitude that different from Judas'?

And if Jesus hungers with the children on the garbage dumps of Rio de Janeiro, and I am unwilling to share from the abundance I have; if Jesus is with those who have to drink polluted water while the good water is diverted to the resorts in their countries, and I don't say something about it; if Jesus is with the people dying in the South, and I am not beating down the doors of my government to get them to stop this genocide – if I am not willing to do anything and everything I can for the lost, the last, the least in our world, then aren't I betraying the very One who I say I want to live in my heart?

The disturbing news of the Passion story, I thought, is how much I resemble Judas. But the good news is that, like Judas, Jesus will honour me by feeding me at his table on Maundy Thursday; and then, as he did for Judas, he will go out and die for me so that, like Judas, I might be saved.

Holy Saturday:
what were they doing today?

Cleaning toilets
trying to forget
their dreams
draining away?

Maybe Peter wished
he was home
eating Passover
leftovers,
trying to find
a way
out of his
wilderness?

*Did Joanna
have her Saturday list:
groceries to buy,
errands to run,
a soccer game? ...*

*Were Herod and Pilate
nursing hangovers,
out too late last night
hitting every pub
on the Street of Tears
until they got
thrown out at the
Last Station?*

*Were children
being shushed by
fear-ridden parents,
told
to stop playing
'Soldiers and messiahs'?*

*Did the angels
tiptoe
around heaven
afraid
to speak too
loudly,
wondering
what with the Word*

*God was doing
behind that stone?*

What were they doing today ...

*before God
yanked the legs
out
from under
death?*

Thom M Shuman

Easter Sunday sermon from Iona Abbey

Feminist theologian and poet Nicola Slee led Holy Week on Iona in 2016.

Nearly 30 years ago, I was on my way to Iona but only got as far as Oban. Early in the morning, when I was due to get the ferry, I received a phone call telling me that my youngest brother Malcolm had been in a severe car accident and was critically ill in Plymouth Hospital.

The 12-hour journey from Oban to Plymouth was perhaps the longest of my life. I was desperate to get to the hospital, yet terrified of what I might find. What kind of state would my brother's battered body be in? How would the members of my family be bearing up? What might the coming days hold? The thought that Malcolm might die was unbearable. But if he were to survive, what kind of life would he have? He had sustained a massive blow to the head and the prognosis was not good. We were told that he might be blind, might never walk again, might not talk or know us, and that the damage to his personality could be profound.

Days of exhausting waiting followed, keeping vigil by his bed. We endlessly rehearsed the details of what had happened, anxiously consulted medics to chart his progress, tried to comfort and reassure each other. For several weeks, Malcolm remained in a deep coma. Then, quite without warning, came a day which I will remember for the rest of my life. I came into the hospital ward where Malcolm was lying unconscious. I did what I'd done countless times: walked up to him, touched his arm and spoke to him. Without moving or waking from unconsciousness, he spoke my name, as if it were the most natural thing in the world. 'Hello, Nicola.' The sound of his voice was a moment of pure and wholly unexpected joy. It was the first sign we'd all been desperately hoping for – not only that he could talk, that he knew me but, more significantly, that he was still recognisably the person we knew and loved; that the bonds of our relation to him had not been severed irretrievably.

Gradually, over weeks and months, that first sign was followed by others, as my brother began to move his body, to talk more, to recover consciousness, to sit up and eat. Later again, when the bandages around his head were removed, he could see, and later still he recovered his capacity to walk. Piece by piece, the old Malcolm was restored to us.

Or so we thought. We so desperately needed and wanted him to be exactly as he had been before. We wanted the miracle of a full return, a total erasure of damage and the wound. I now see that we were in denial, and it has taken years for us to recognise and accept the much more complex reality of Malcolm's healing – a real but nevertheless partial healing, which has left him blessed but wounded, a vulnerable adult with personality damage who needs a good deal of support. We have had to accept that he has changed – and so have we. We can't go back to how it was before.

Was it something like this for Mary Magdalene on that first Easter morning? John's narrative is a complex one, compressing many stages of a psychological process that might normally take months, if not years, into one brief encounter. Mary comes to the tomb early, in the pre-dawn dark, in a state of extreme grief and desolation. She has accompanied Jesus, with the other women, throughout the long process of his betrayal, trial, scourging and crucifixion, watching him writhe on the cross, powerless to lift a finger to stop the cruelty or to alleviate his suffering. At last, his ordeal is over and his body lies in the tomb, hastily buried before the start of the Sabbath. Mary is desperate to be reunited with that beloved body after the enforced Sabbath curfew, and this seems to be the one thought that drives her.

Coming to the tomb and finding the stone rolled away and no sign of the body, she is completely disoriented and thrown into even greater desolation and agitation. Her longing and need to handle and touch the dead body is refused. She assumes the body has been stolen or removed and runs to Simon Peter and the Beloved Disciple to tell them and to seek their help. There follows a little interlude in which the two male disciples run, pell-mell, to the tomb in a competition to see who will get there first (even *in extremis*, they can't stop behaving like men!). They get there, go into the tomb and discover the linen wrappings lying there – and, strangely, return to their homes. But Mary won't leave. Even though the body isn't there, it's the last place where the body has been and it therefore provides some link, some tenuous connection, back to Jesus.

Weeping by the tomb, she meets the angels who enquire into the cause of her grief. Three times in this passage she speaks of the body of Jesus having been taken away – first to the male disciples, then to the angels and finally to Jesus (though she doesn't know it is him). The irony is that the risen Christ is standing right next to her, but in her grief and fixation on finding the body, she doesn't recognise him. 'Supposing him to be the gardener', she does not yet understand the miracle of transformation that Christ's own body has undergone. Like the grain of wheat that falls into the ground, the dead body of Jesus does not remain as it was but has been transformed into something wholly different and more glorious. It's as if Mary is fumbling about in the dirt looking for the dead husk of seed or grain buried there rather than looking up to see the magnificent Easter lily blooming right in front of her eyes.

It is only when the Risen Christ speaks Mary's name that she finally recognises him. There is an intense, rapturous reunion as she turns to embrace him and responds with an answering cry. Yet this isn't the end of the story, like some final scene in a Hollywood movie where the two lovers clinch in a rose-tinted kiss. There's further to go and yet another twist in the psychological drama.

At the very moment of reunion, Christ recoils from Mary and rejects her touch. 'Do not cling to me,' he says to her. 'Do not hold on to me.'

At the heart of resurrection is rupture and refusal, rather than reunion. There is no return to the garden of innocence for Mary any more than there was for Adam and Eve or there is for us. The way back to some past Paradise is forever barred – whether that be the first flush of love or youthful faith or certainty about our vocation. Resurrection is not return, nor the restoration of an old state of affairs, but a total reorientation to a radically new reality.

'Do not hold on to me … but go to my brothers and sisters …' How traumatic was it for Mary to hear these words and act on them? Like the process of birth for the newborn, she must have experienced this rejection as a terrifying and deathly expulsion. Yet this is what Resurrection demanded of her – and of us. Christ commands us to go, to leave the safe womb/garden and to risk the loss of all we have known.

> 'Yet, as Mary obeys the Lord's command, she discovers the deeper miracle and truth of the resurrection which, until now, she could not know. She finds that Christ is there, wherever she goes, the living one present with her, within her, beside her and before her, not simply in the particular space and time of the garden encounter, but released in the world everywhere …'[1]

Christ is risen, raised into a new and glorious physical body, the transformed body of which Paul speaks in Corinthians. He is not a mere resuscitated corpse, nor is he raised like Lazarus to resume his previous life. His risen body is resplendent, glorious – as a spring daffodil or lily is more resplendent than the bulb from which it springs – but his body also bears the scars, the wounds of his crucifixion, now glorified – a sign of hope to us that our scars, too, may become sites of transformation and healing.

The risen Christ is the same and yet different from Jesus of Nazareth (which is why, in all the resurrection stories, the disciples fail to recognise him). Jesus of Nazareth had a specific, limited, historical identity – male, Jewish-Palestinian, young, able-bodied (at least until disabled on the cross). The risen Christ is no longer confined by these limits, and may come to us in any number of unfamiliar guises: as female, transgendered; as lesbian or gay; with an African, or Syrian or Belgian face; as atheist, or Muslim or Sikh; as newborn and aged; as blind or limping or mentally wounded. For we are now the body of Christ/Christa, and touch his body, her body – at last – in one another, and in the bodies of all we meet, as well as the lovely body of the earth itself, the air, sky, sun, moon, water, fire, plants and animals.

So, sisters and brothers, fellow earth creatures, let us go out from the garden, and from this beautiful island, full of joy and expectation; willing to leave behind the Jesus we thought we knew in order to meet the unknown Christ awaiting us wherever we travel in the world. Let us return to our homes, our workplaces, our cities and villages, in the danger and the risk of resurrection faith. For Christ has died, Christ is risen, Christ will come again – and again and again. Alleluia!

Nicola Slee

Source:
1. From *Easter Garden*, Nicola Slee, Collins Fount, 1990, p.147

Love that breaks open stone
Poems for Easter Sunday

Easter morning: Too early

I have folded you away
in a mess of rotting tree
I have laid you down
on lilacs

I have covered you
smothered you
liberally anointed you
wept for you
dropped tears on you
filled day and night
with grief for you

I have laid you down
in scented lilacs

My garden

The knocking
had kept me awake
night after night.

Sometimes it was gentle.
Mostly it was
as if my very

heart was the door,
and I trembled lest the wood splinter
under the force.

Life had taught me
to be wary. Perhaps,
with the
pillow over my
head I could
shut out the sound.
And the fear.

Night after night.

And then it stopped.
The knocking. It was no more.
Night after empty night.
Sometimes, in my dreams, I thought
I heard its echo. And I ran to the door
and flung it open, panting, laughing,
eager.

'Here I am.'

But there was no one
in my garden, walking
in the cool of the day.

And the earth, where once
I had sown companion
plants, foxgloves, marigolds

and forget-me-nots,
had been cleared. And in places
there was a dusting
of salt,
where someone
had been crying.
'My garden,'
I screamed,
as the wood splintered.
'What have you done
to my garden?'

That was the first day.

A considerate rising

Not a wild, reckless rising
but domestic
tidy,
the strips of linen
folded
for life's
next passing guest.

And somehow I cannot
see you standing
there, smiling, as
the angels clear the
mess.

For you are a
maker of mess, blood-
soiler of sheets, smearing
with sweat and
with vinegar.
Yours is a body embalmed,
staining with oil and
with spices.

And yours is a body
fluid with the calm
rhythm of courtesy.

The women find no ordinary
work awaiting in
your wake.

Daffodils

For the first time
the daffodils do not bring
me cheerfulness,
their nodding yellow heads
incongruent, stubborn,
sunshine at the wrong
end of winter.

It is wartime.
The earth wrestles against
the seedcorn.

The ploughed fields
may or may not see harvest.
There are old gun emplacements
on the clifftops, looking
across the estuary to
the nuclear power plant.
Around their concrete bases
the same jaundiced flowers.
Spring's heralds or signs of
our fear?

I do not know whether to fight
or to flee. I do not know if the
east wind will spread pollen
or freeze away the first hope of life.

On the borders of Europe they are
herding people into cages and sending them
back to the bombs.

On the borders of this field
there are daffodils, nodding away
as the bodies wash again, out to sea.

In the cracks

It is in the cracks that the wild things grow
bugle purpling over the stone, ox-eyes
looking fearlessly into the sun
for the light

that will one day wither their sight.
Droplets of gold vetch, stretch.

She was right first time. You are the
gardener after all, with a love
that breaks open stone, and hands too
freshly cracked
for her to touch.

Only the desperate and doubting
may press the red petal palms
and see the pollen stain their fingertips.

Alison Swinfen

Night sight
On working as a street pastor

'Take us outside, O Christ, outside holiness …'
– George MacLeod

I went into the city that is my home,
to be amongst those whom I usually wouldn't see.
The revellers and partygoers,
those forging new relationships, or escaping old ones;
those who sleep behind derelict churches,
and those who relieve themselves in alleyways.
Burly ones at doorways, and uniformed ones patrolling in twos,
we walked amongst them all.

Our clothing marked us out.
Others too were in costume, identifying their role, their purpose.
We were all there for our own reasons,
looking for something.
I, to deliberately place myself outside:
outside my comfort zone, my familiar experiences,
outside the people I choose to surround myself with,
alongside others.
I found open doorways I had never before noticed
leading to bright, loud places;
and the locked doorways I more commonly frequent
I found I share with others, who shelter there by night.
I found revelations of authenticity
normally repressed by light and sobriety,
and openness of hearts
touched by simple kindness.

To some we gave Spikeys*, to others blankets,
for some we bought coffee, to others we gave water.
We listened to a story of an abusive marriage,
and many stories of 'boyfriend's gone off with best friend'.
We handed out flip-flops and plasters,
and collected discarded bottles and glasses.
And I found I belong there too.

Elaine Gisbourne

*A plastic stopper that prevents drinks from being spiked.

Invisible guests

John McCall has lived in Taiwan for 20 years, teaching at seminaries there and in China, and working with church leaders in Asia.

They are present in most developed countries. You may not see them but they pick the crops, sweep the floors, care for the children and elderly, build infrastructure, labour in factories, cook and serve.

They often have to leave their home countries and families in order to find a job. Much of the money which they earn they send back to their families. I've seen them in the fern fields of central Florida. I've seen them pushing a stroller with someone else's baby in the Upper West Side of New York City. I see them in Taipei walking alongside and assisting someone else's grandmother. I hear them on the subway talking in their mother tongue on a cell phone.

Recently I had the opportunity to travel to Malaysia to speak to leaders and members from twenty churches of the Presbyterian Church in Malaysia. Malaysia is a fascinating country with three main people groups: the Malays, who are Muslim, the Chinese, who worship traditional folk gods and a good number who are Christian, and the Indians, who are Hindu, Sikh or worship other Indian gods. While Malaysians do not necessarily have total racial harmony, it is striking to see all these different folk living together in peace. But in addition to these three people groups, there are also a number of other south-east Asians who have come to Malaysia to find work.

I was staying in a simple hotel in the city of Kluang while I was teaching and preaching. During the five days I was there, I didn't see another Westerner. Located next to the hotel was a BBQ restaurant owned by a Chinese-Malaysian. There are a number of folk from other countries working at this restaurant. Each evening, as I returned to the hotel, I would talk with these young men, and during the week, as they were finishing their jobs of sweeping and mopping and preparing the hot pepper sauce for the next day, they would offer me a glass of tea and tell me of their lives.

I got to know Iman from Indonesia. He is a Muslim and speaks Malay so has no trouble with communication in Malaysia. He told me how his parents cried when he prepared to leave them to go to Malaysia. He is a bright young man with a light in his eyes. Another young man, Nini, is from Myanmar, a country which is experiencing tremendous change as a new government begins to govern there. Nini has nine brothers and sisters and told me that when he was growing up there would be three brothers in one bed. He is a Buddhist. The third young man, Raz, is from Nepal. His eyes lit up when I mentioned the Himalayas. Raz is a Hindu.

Each evening these three young men welcomed me to their place of work. They would put their mops aside and sit with me. Their boss also seemed interested in what we were talking about and several times he joined us at the table. They told me of their dreams and lives. One showed me pictures of his Vietnamese girlfriend.

On my last night in Kluang, I told them that I would be leaving the next day. Iman and Nini asked me what time I would be leaving. They then told me that they had a day off the next day and wanted to come and say goodbye.

So the next morning I checked out of the hotel and went downstairs, and saw them standing there. They had dressed up in their finest and Nini had brought his Vietnamese girlfriend so that I could meet her. We took pictures and laughed together.

I wanted to bless them in some way, but also wanted to be sensitive to them. They knew that I was a pastor and had been speaking at the church in town.

So I asked them if I could offer a prayer of blessing for them. We held hands, and I prayed for each of them. A music teacher from our seminary in Taipei, who was also one of the speakers at the church gathering, was there and joined in the circle. The two of us sang a song of blessing for them. They smiled and clapped. It was a wonderful moment of connection.

As one of the Malaysian pastors picked us up and we waved goodbye from the car, I wondered about the future of these young people. One's birthplace and family economic situation can affect so much about our futures. I prayed silently for them as we drove away. In our divided world, it was such a joy to get to know a Muslim, a Buddhist and a Hindu and to share tea together. I felt as if Christ was the unseen guest at that table. I don't know how God will use our time together, but I know that God was present in our meeting.

John McCall

The ten Beatitudes

My French wife and I, she of Huguenot stock, take our holidays in the Cévennes. There, in 1878, in the land of her ancestors, Robert Louis Stevenson made his famous journey with a donkey. It's wonderful to have connections with a part of France that has been so shaped in its identity by a Scottish writer. At the little commune of Saint-Germain-de-Calberte I talked to David, an elected councillor. I asked, 'What did Stevenson do for you?' And he answered, 'He gave us back our history.'

This past summer we spent time there down by the river. I found myself thinking about spiritual teaching stories. Like the river rolling on, how do they find new life for the present day? What prompted this reflection, was that in the previous week I'd heard somebody ask a question. 'Why do we hear much about the Ten Commandments, but little of the Beatitudes?'

It seemed to me that, especially for the modern world, we have a marketing problem. The Ten Commandments have been packaged to punch out a message. For whatever reasons, not so the Beatitudes.

First, consider the Commandments. They are found in slightly differing forms in both Exodus 20 and Deuteronomy 5. Some scholars reckon they can actually be broken down into nearly twenty commandments. For example, how many proud anglers who might be sticklers for the Ten Commandments pay attention to a subclause of the injunction against making graven images? How many, when submitting snapshots of their trophy catches to the *Stornoway Gazette*, remember that the text says: 'Thou shalt not make unto thee … any likeness of any thing … that is in the water under the earth' (Exodus 20:4)?

A point not to be taken too seriously? Well, that depends on your era and theology. In *The Men of Lewis*, a classic text about the evangelical revivals of the northern Outer Hebrides, the Rev Norman Macfarlane remarked that one evangelical, 'like many worthy men who regarded photographers as notorious breakers of the Second Commandment … would never listen to any appeal made for his portrait.'

My point is not to have a dig at conservative Christian anglers. Not even to open a window on an age when the 'selfie' would have been considered the height of godless vanity. My point is simply to show that the 'ten' Commandments are a simplified representation, a marketing package, as might be said, of more complex and nuanced material. A summary that has been created down through Christian tradition with the number ten chosen as an aide-memoire.

If so for the Commandments, why not for the Beatitudes? We find them spread over two gospels. There are twelve of them in total, eight of them in Matthew 5 and four in Luke 6. The messaging is more scattered than the Commandments. There are gaps, overlap and repetition such as, if you try trotting out the Twelve Beatitudes, you end up falling over yourself. They just don't sit very neatly together.

That said, some of the apparent repetition carries important nuances. Consider the near-duplication of 'Blessed are the poor …' (Luke 6:20) and 'Blessed are the poor in spirit …' (Matthew 5:3). These days, freely available online tools like Bible Hub make it easy to delve into the original Greek. *Ptōchoi* quite plainly means poor in the sense of economic destitution; so poor means poor and Luke is talking about material poverty. Matthew, however, uses the same word, but clearly as a metaphor by specifying 'poor in spirit'. This can be read as offering us two distinct Beatitudes. One for the material world, the other for the spiritual. Both matter. If you go only with Luke, you get an overly materialistic spirituality. If only with Matthew, an overly otherworldly spirituality. While we don't need to labour the point, the same goes for those who hunger. Luke leaves hunger as hunger. Matthew treats the hunger (and thirst) as being for righteousness.

Sitting by the river in the Cévennes that summer's day in France, I played with the Beatitudes using apps on my phone. I had translations in both the King James Version and the Revised Standard Version (Catholic Edition). These I distilled down into a decalogue – a set of ten statements – that felt satisfying and usable in teaching contexts. Others might make their own selection. Some might feel that no selection should be made. But in case it's helpful, here's what I came up with:

'And Jesus lifted up his eyes on his disciples, and said:

1. 'Blessed are you poor, for yours is the kingdom of God.
2. 'Blessed are the poor in spirit, for theirs is the kingdom of heaven.
3. 'Blessed are you that hunger now, for you shall be satisfied.
4. 'Blessed are you that weep now, for you shall laugh.
5. 'Blessed are they that mourn, for they shall be comforted.
6. 'Blessed are the meek, for they shall inherit the earth.
7. 'Blessed are the merciful, for they shall obtain mercy.
8. 'Blessed are the pure in heart, for they shall see God.
9. 'Blessed are the peacemakers, for they shall be called [daughters and] sons of God.
10. 'Blessed are those who are persecuted for righteousness' sake, for theirs is the kingdom of heaven.'

1: Lk. 6:20
2: Mt. 5:3
3: Lk. 6:21a
4: Lk. 6:21b
5: Mt. 5:4
6: Mt. 5:5
7: Mt. 5:7
8: Mt. 5:8
9: Mt. 5:9
10: Mt. 5:10

Alastair McIntosh

Suggestion for contemplation and prayer (Ed.):

Write the 10 Beatitudes on a 'prayer card' and carry this around with you throughout Holy Week, or after. Reflect on the Beatitudes, or on a single Beatitude, throughout the journey of your day. You might like to say this prayer, by Ruth Burgess, to finish:

Holy merciful God,
write the values of the Beatitudes
into my heart and life
and help me to seek your face
and happily walk in your ways.
Amen

Ruth Burgess (adapted)

The incredible love of God in Christ

All of us who are prepared to give thought to the last week of Jesus Christ's earthly life should make space to let awe and gratitude penetrate our beings. In the end we need to lay down the reading matter, put aside our specs – and open our beings to the incredible love of God in Christ, so that we are given time to be transfigured by the love as it is absorbed.

Imagine the whole universe as an amphitheatre in which God the Lord works out his will for the created order, inviting human beings to undertake a kind of junior partnership in bringing all life to its fulfilment.

Central to the hope for the universe is a love figure, Jesus Christ. Take two perspectives on his part, and see how they relate to one another.

The first is Paul's cosmic context of operation: *'He is the image of the invisible God, the firstborn of all creation, for in him all things in heaven and on earth were created – things visible and invisible, including thrones, dominions, rulers, powers: all things have been created through him and for him. He himself is before all things and it is in him that all things hold together'* (Colossians 1:15–17).

Pause on Paul's words. Take time to caress them with the fingertips of your mind to let their hidden glories be released. Revel in the fact that what is definitive of the universe and its purpose is not some obscure shaping force but the dynamic of a God of love who, in Christ, is the light of the world. Revel, and revel again, and teach others to revel in the light of the world, who is before all things, above all things, life's Alpha and Omega.

Now turn to the second perspective given in biblical narrative of Jesus' last week of life: Jesus seems to be submerged under the weight of plots and plans of other people, a scapegoat of their aspirations, their hopes, fears. He does not seem to have an agenda. He is merely an item on the agendas of others; humiliated, mocked, given a crown – but of thorns – derided as a pretender, a saviour of others who cannot save himself, a huge disappointment to followers on the Emmaus road: *'We had hoped that he was the one to redeem Israel'*. A failure!

Who is in charge of the situation?

Authority is shown in the ride into Jerusalem, fulfilling the prophecy of one *'triumphant and victorious'* and yet humble and riding on a donkey.

Authority is shown in the overturning of the tables of the money-changers in the Temple – *'a house of prayer for all nations'* turned into a den of robbers. By sheer authority *'he would not allow anyone to carry anything through the temple'*, thus interrupting the worship which superstition suggested had to proceed in an unbroken line of development.

Twelve legions of angels, who could have come to Jesus' rescue, were confined to barracks – even the experience of God-forsakenness could not break Jesus' resolution to provide for the Father a form of humanity which the Father could trust to shun escape routes and stay faithful to the end, which was marked by the cry: *'It is finished.'* Assignment fulfilled! A humanity made available which stands up to testing to the limit, gives hope for humanity in all ages.

Take time to look, one by one, at the humiliations, the tortures, the rejections which Jesus let himself in for, and marvel, marvel at the self-giving love of God in Christ who will go to such lengths for our sake …

In the end we need to lay down the reading matter and open our beings to the incredible love of God in Christ, so that we are given time to be transfigured by love as it is absorbed.

Ian M Fraser

Sources and acknowledgements

THE HOLY BIBLE, NEW INTERNATIONAL VERSION®, NIV® Copyright © 1973, 1978, 1984, 2011 by Biblica, Inc.® Used by permission. All rights reserved worldwide

Passages from NRSV copyright 1989, Division of Christian Education of the National Council of the Churches of Christ in the United States of America. Used by permission. All rights reserved.

The New Jerusalem Bible, published and copyright 1985 by Darton, Longman & Todd Ltd and Les Editions du Cerf, and used by permission of the publishers.

'Prayers for the journey to Easter (from Maundy Thursday to Easter Sunday)', by Elaine Gisbourne, Wild Goose Publications download

'This is my child', by Anna Briggs, from *Coracle*: the magazine of the Iona Community, autumn 2015, Neil Paynter (Ed.)

'May peace prevail', Lyn Ma and Neil Squires, from *Coracle*: the magazine of the Iona Community, autumn 2016, Neil Paynter (Ed.)

'Prayers on crucifixion', by David Rhodes, from *It Wasn't the Nails*, David Rhodes, Wild Goose Publications download

'Take us back: Good Friday worship on the words from the Cross', by David McNeish, Wild Goose Publications download

'Your life in us: Prayers on the seven words from the Cross', by Peter Millar, Wild Goose Publications download

'We will tread the earth lightly: A service of lamentation to liberate us for action', by Chris Polhill, Wild Goose Publications download

'Easter Sunday sermon from Iona Abbey', by Nicola Slee, from *Coracle*: the magazine of the Iona Community, summer 2016, Neil Paynter (Ed.)

'Night sight', by Elaine Gisbourne, from *Living Letters of the Word: Readings & Meditations from the Iona Community,* Neil Paynter (Ed.), Wild Goose Publications, 2012

'Invisible guests', by John McCall, from *Coracle*: the magazine of the Iona Community, summer 2016, Neil Paynter (Ed.)

'Holy merciful God …', by Ruth Burgess, from *Candles and Conifers: Resources for All Saints' to Advent,* Wild Goose Publications, 2005 (prayer adapted)

About the authors

Anna Briggs is a member of the Iona Community.

Ruth Burgess is a member of the Iona Community and the author of several books (Wild Goose Publications).

David J.M.Coleman is a URC minister, digital artist and member of the Iona Community.

Ian M Fraser has been a pastor-labourer in heavy industry, a parish minister, Warden of Scottish Churches House, an Executive Secretary of the World Council of Churches, and Dean and Head of the Department of Mission at Selly Oak Colleges, Birmingham. He is the author of numerous books, including *Strange Fire*, *The Way Ahead: Grown-up Christians*, and *Reinventing Theology*, which is used as a standard theological sourcebook throughout the world. Ian is one of the original members of the Iona Community who helped George MacLeod to rebuild the common life and the Abbey buildings on the isle of Iona. Throughout his life Ian has travelled the world, alone and with his wife, Margaret, visiting basic Christian communities. He has walked alongside slum dwellers in India and Haiti; Nicaraguan and Cuban revolutionaries; priests, nuns and catechists facing arrest and/or death in Central and South America; and small farming and fishing communities in the Philippines.

Elaine Gisbourne lives in the north-west of England where it is usually wet but always beautiful. She shares her home with her husband, three daughters, two dogs and four hens. Elaine volunteers as a Street Pastor in Lancaster: it is frequently cold, often wet, but always inspiring. Elaine loves being taken by surprise by finding God in unexpected places.

Lyn Ma teaches ESOL to refugees at Glasgow Clyde College. She has been working with asylum seekers and refugees for over 15 years. She is a former volunteer on Iona and at the Corrymeela Community.

John McCall has been an associate member of the Iona Community since 1984. He serves with the Presbyterian Church in Taiwan, teaching at seminaries in both Taiwan and China. He also leads groups of Taiwanese pastors in spiritual formation groups, encouraging them to dream God's Easter dream for the churches and people of Taiwan.

Alastair McIntosh is a Quaker and an associate of the Iona Community. He is the author of several books, including *Poacher's Pilgrimage: An Island Journey* (Birlinn), *Spiritual Activism: Leadership as Service* (Green Books), *Parables of Northern Seed: Anthology from BBC's Thought for the Day* (Wild Goose Publications), and *Soil and Soul: People versus Corporate Power* (Aurum Press).

David McNeish is an Iona Community member living and working in the West Mainland of Orkney with his wife and three growing children. He is minister of Milestone Community Church, chairs Orkney Pilgrimage, the group behind the establishment of the St Magnus Way, and enjoys writing songs.

Peter Millar is a former warden of Iona Abbey, who has worked in India, Glasgow, Africa and Australia. He is the author of several books, including *An Iona Prayer Book* (Canterbury Press), *Finding Hope Again* (Canterbury Press), *A Time to Mend* (Wild Goose Publications) and *Our Hearts Still Sing* (Wild Goose Publications). He is a soul friend to many.

Mike Mineter: 'After many years as an associate member of the Iona Community, I joined as a full member in 2013. I'm a Roman Catholic, a sea kayaker and a computing specialist working in climate science at the University of Edinburgh. In November 2016 I made my second trip to Israel/Palestine. On the first trip a year earlier I had spent time in Nazareth and then two days walking to the Sea of Galilee, before joining a Church's pilgrimage to the holy sites. In this second trip I wanted to get a little deeper into current realities, and visited several groups that were creatively seeking a better future: Kairos Palestine (www.kairospalestine.ps), Sabeel (www.friendsofsabeel.org.uk), Tent of Nations (www.tentofnations.org), and Wi'am (www.alaslah.org).'

Paul Nicolson is a long-time campaigner against poverty and injustice. He is the founder of Zacchaeus 2000 Trust (http://z2k.org/) and Taxpayers Against Poverty (http://taxpayersagainstpoverty.org.uk) in Tottenham, and is an associate of the Iona Community.

Marie Pattison is director of Katherine House (www.katherinehousefcj.org), a retreat house in Salford owned by the Faithful Companions of Jesus. She is churchwarden at Sacred Trinity Church. Believing that faith and justice go hand in hand she has campaigned with Church Action on Poverty for a number of years (www.church-poverty.org.uk).

Neil Paynter is an editor, writer and late-night piano player, who lives with his partner Helen, his mum and Stevie the cat in a flat in Biggar, Scotland. Previously he worked in night shelters for the homeless in Canada and the UK.

Chris Polhill is a member of the Iona Community and one of the first women to be ordained a priest in the Church of England. She is the author of a number of books and resources, including *A Heart for Creation: Worship Resources and Reflections on the Environment* (Wild Goose Publications). She and her husband, John, run Reflection Gardens in Cannock Wood (http://homepages.phonecoop.coop/reflections/intro.htm), which illustrates connections between care for the environment and the Christian spiritual journey.

Katharine M Preston is an ecumenical lay preacher and writer, concentrating on issues of social justice and climate change. She and her husband, John Bingham, are active associates of the Iona Community, living on a farm in Essex, New York.

Brian Quail: Prisoner No. 133799 Quail, Brian Michael, religion R.C., born 24/03/1938, former Principal Teacher Latin Greek Russian, father of seven, grandfather to fifteen, member Pax Christi, Iona Community, Scottish CND, SCANA, Catholic Worker, Trident Ploughshares, into Russian icons, wildflowers, Bach, curry, reggae, Gaelic, Ravi Shankar, poetry, Gregorian plainchant, beer, history, Russian Orthodoxy, the Georgian language, the Shroud of Turin, Russian Church music, Bob Marley, daffodils, dancing, Dostoyevsky and Mozart.

David Rhodes worked as a national newspaper journalist, before his ordination as an Anglican priest. In the 1990s he joined the ecumenical project Faith in Leeds and began running his innovative 'retreats on the streets' to help Christians make the vital connection between their faith and social justice issues. He is the author of several books, including *Finding Mr Goldman: A Parable*, and *Faith in Dark Places* (SPCK).

Thom M Shuman serves as a semi-retired pastor. Committed to non-violence, he supports justice for immigrants, refugees and people with mental illness. He is an associate of the Iona Community, and the author of several books and downloads, including *The Soft Petals of Grace* (Wild Goose Publications).

Nicola Slee is Director of Research at the Queen's Foundation for Ecumenical Theological Education (www.queens.ac.uk), and the author of many books, including *Doing December Differently*, with Rosie Miles (Wild Goose Publications), and *Praying Like a Woman* (SPCK).

Neil Squires is currently Chief Exec of Harmeny Education Trust, in Edinburgh, which provides residential and day education for children who have experienced severe trauma and loss in their early years, through abuse and neglect. He has been a member of the Iona Community since 1997.

Alison Swinfen is UNESCO Professor of Refugee integration through languages and the arts, University of Glasgow; Co-convener of Glasgow Refugee, Asylum and Migration Network (GRAMNet): https://gramnet.wordpress.com; and a member of the Iona Community.

Bonnie Thurston resigned a professorship and chair in New Testament to live quietly in her home state of West Virginia. She is the author of academic works (many of which focus on practical application of scripture), books on spirituality and five collections of poetry. She volunteers at a food pantry in Wheeling, WV, USA.

Stephen Wright works as a spiritual director for the Sacred Space Foundation (www.sacredspace.org.uk) in Cumbria. Before this he had a long and distinguished nursing career in academia and the National Health Service, the Royal College of Nursing and as a consultant to the World Health Organisation. He lives with his partner in the Lake District, deepening service and spiritual practice, participating in his local church community, taking care of his organic garden and enjoying grandfatherhood.

Wild Goose Publications is part of the Iona Community:

- An ecumenical movement of men and women from different walks of life and different traditions in the Christian church
- Committed to the gospel of Jesus Christ, and to following where that leads, even into the unknown
- Engaged together, and with people of goodwill across the world, in acting, reflecting and praying for justice, peace and the integrity of creation
- Convinced that the inclusive community we seek must be embodied in the community we practise

Together with our staff, we are responsible for:

- Our islands residential centres of Iona Abbey, the MacLeod Centre on Iona, and Camas Adventure Centre on the Ross of Mull

and in Glasgow:
- The administration of the Community
- Our work with young people
- Our publishing house, Wild Goose Publications
- Our association in the revitalising of worship with the Wild Goose Resource Group

The Iona Community was founded in Glasgow in 1938 by George MacLeod, minister, visionary and prophetic witness for peace, in the context of the poverty and despair of the Depression. Its original task of rebuilding the monastic ruins of Iona Abbey became a sign of hopeful rebuilding of community in Scotland and beyond. Today, we are about 250 Members, mostly in Britain, and 1500 Associate Members, with 1400 Friends worldwide. Together and apart, 'we follow the light we have, and pray for more light'.

For information on the Iona Community contact:
The Iona Community, 21 Carlton Court,
Glasgow G5 9JP, UK. Phone: 0141 429 7281
e-mail: admin@iona.org.uk; web: www.iona.org.uk

For enquiries about visiting Iona, please contact:
Iona Abbey, Isle of Iona, Argyll PA76 6SN, UK. Phone: 01681 700404
e-mail: ionacomm@iona.org.uk

Wild Goose Publications, the publishing house of the Iona Community established in the Celtic Christian tradition of Saint Columba, produces books, e-books, CDs and digital downloads on:

- holistic spirituality
- social justice
- political and peace issues
- healing
- innovative approaches to worship
- song in worship, including the work of the Wild Goose Resource Group
- material for meditation and reflection

For more information:

Wild Goose Publications
The Iona Community
21 Carlton Court, Glasgow, G5 9JP, UK

Tel. +44 (0)141 429 7281
e-mail: admin@ionabooks.com

or visit our website at
www.ionabooks.com
for details of all our products and online sales